More Abundant
LIFE

100 Days to Start or Restart
your Christian Walk

- Lawrence H. Phipps

Selected drawings by Heather and Lauren Phipps

Scripture quotations marked NIV are from the Holy Bible, *New International Version* © copyright 1973, 1978, 1984 by International Bible Society.

Scripture quotations marked KJV are from the *King James Version* of the Bible.

Scripture quotations marked NKJ are from the *New King James* version.

Scripture quotations marked NJB are from the *New Jerusalem Bible*. © 1979, 1980, 1982, Thomas Nelson, Inc., Publishers. Used by permission.

Churches may obtain additional copies of this book at ItsLifeMinistry.com (click on "Bookstore"), or by calling It's Life Ministry, LLC at (334) 328-5232; or email lawrence.phipps@itslifeministry.com.

Printed by Wells Printing, Montgomery, Alabama, in the United States of America

TABLE OF CONTENTS

The Writer

After thirty-six years as a pastor, Dr. Lawrence H. Phipps and his wife Karen moved by faith in 2013 to begin ItsLifeMinistry.com. He left the fast growing First Baptist Church of Enterprise, Alabama, in 1994 to begin Vaughn Forest Church in Montgomery, Alabama. In nearly twenty years as Vaughn Forest's pastor, the church baptized 2313 individuals. The fast growth of the church led Dr. Phipps to seek materials for new believers. After discovering that all books and brochures for new believers assumed a certain level of biblical and church knowledge, he was led to write a book that assumes the reader does not even know the Bible has a table of contents. More Abundant Life is designed to help every believer get his or her spiritual feet on the ground.

Dr. Lawrence H. Phipps has a BA degree from Auburn University, Auburn, Alabama. He holds master of divinity and doctor of ministry degrees from The Southern Baptist Theological Seminary. He has served as pastor of churches in both Kentucky and Alabama.

In 1989 Phipps began discipling individuals through the process of Evangelism Explosion. He became a Senior Clinic teacher for E.E. International and later a Lead Teacher for the FAITH Strategy for evangelizing and equipping new believers. In the FAITH ministry, he authored the book *Praying in FAITH* for LifeWay Christian Resources. In 2001 Phipps' involvement in the Sunday School led him, with the help of Daniel Edmonds, to author the book *Growing Sunday School/ Small Group TEAMS*. Phipps then wrote the evangelism-discipleship process *It's LIFE*, which guides churches to involve believers and unbelievers in Sunday Bible study, or weekly small groups.

Acknowledgments

My greatest appreciation goes to my heavenly Father, Jesus and His Holy Spirit for giving me life, breath, life everlasting and a call to preach the gospel. My greatest thanks on earth go to my wife Karen, and to my daughters Heather and Lauren for allowing me to borrow some Daddy-Daughter time to write.

I appreciate Dr. Rob Jackson who, at the time of the first printing, was a member who provided my inspiration for one-on-one discipling. I am grateful for many people at Vaughn Forest Church who gave me the support and encouragement to develop a step-by-step plan for making disciples. I thank Becky Peavy, my assistant for many years, who used the publishing program and provided the expertise to organize the book and my mother-in-law, Evie Lou McMoy who used her expertise as an English teacher to edit the book.

The worth of *More Abundant LIFE* has been seen in the lives of those who worked through the book and began to grow. Those who have grown to become soul-winners and disciple-makers are to be commended.

I dedicate this fourth edition of *More Abundant LIFE* to Drs. Richard Cunningham and Howard Cobble, 1983 D.Min. faculty and field supervisors, respectively. Both worked diligently to teach me how to write. I am glad they challenged me and did not grow weary. I also want to dedicate this edition to Dr. Isaac B. McDonald, my "dad in ministry". He has been a true friend and confidant.

Preface

Jesus told those of us who follow Him to make disciples. Sometimes we focus on one's decision to follow Christ and forget to help him/her to grow as a believer. We can see many people come to Christ, follow Christ in baptism, register for a small group, but hardly grow. Unfortunately, disciple-makers often assume new believers have a certain amount of knowledge. This book covers the basics so that if you are a new believer you will have a foundation for learning and growing. If you have been a Christian but need to re-start your Christian walk, then *More Abundant LIFE* (MAL) is for you.

 MAL is written to help believers realize that everything we should know and do falls into one of seven categories. I call these pillars. The foundation for Christians is Jesus. He is as wide, deep and strong as you will need. What you build on this foundation is up to you. Your seven pillars are: 1. Prayer; 2. Worship; 3. Witness; 4. Bible study; 5. Discipleship; 6. Fellowship; 7. Service. Virtually everything you will learn from God's word fits into one of these pillars. Having strong pillars will allow you to grow mightily.

This fourth edition of *More Abundant LIFE* can be used by **individuals**, in **Discipleship groups**, or in **Sunday School**. If used in a group, your teacher will be your disciple leader and help you during this journey. Only 2 percent of adult Sunday School members read their lessons weekly. Something needs to change. MAL can be what changes adults from being soakers to servants.

It is important to use the tools listed on page 9. They will maximize your study and growth. Readers will learn how to establish a "priority time" with God. Disciples who complete their journal each day will see growth that will be beyond that which those who simply listen or read see. The author's goal is to help the reader produce a diary that one day will help him or her to understand how God has worked powerfully in his or her life.

The fourth edition follows the pattern of the second and third editions. The book is written in a seven-day format. Once you get past the first day, suggested to be on Sunday, there will be **five** days of new information (Monday-Friday), **one** day of review (Saturday), and **one** day to focus on worship and learning from the worship experience (Sunday). Before you begin, receive this prayer. Write your name in each blank below and then read this prayer that I prayed for you:

"Father, thank You for placing this book in the hands of _____. With You there are no accidents. You have guided _____ to this moment in time for the purpose of growing and helping others to grow. Lord, protect the daily time this study will take. I pray that You will put up a wall of protection so that nothing will be able to stop _____'s spiritual growth. Fill_____ with Your Holy Spirit, because Your Spirit will do all the teaching. Bless_____ for being willing to spend time with You. Jesus, I pray this in your name and according to Your will, amen.   -Lawrence

How to Use *MAL* in Sunday School or Small Groups

Sunday School or small groups should always be open. If you enter a small group that is using this book, then begin by completing Week One. After completing Week One, the reader can join his/her group where they are. Once the quarter is over, return to Week Two and complete all weeks not previously completed.

Read what others are saying about *More Abundant LIFE*

"The pastor at my church gave my husband and me both a copy of More Abundant Life the day we were saved;11/5/13. This book has been wonderful in helping me gain a better understanding of what it means to be a Christian. Thank you for writing this book. I am 25 years old and this is my first time to really get involved in church and actually look forward to Wednesdays and Sundays. God Bless you!"

-Lauren Y., Tuscaloosa, AL

"Just a quick note to let you know how helpful *More Abundant LIFE* has been to both my pastor and me. My sister gave me your book after hearing of my salvation. My pastor at GLBC and I had been looking for a book that would get me "up to speed", as well as give me tools to reference scripture in times of need. As soon as I introduced Bro. Eric to your book, he went to your web site and purchased a copy. I am following the lessons and Bro. Eric is guiding my learning. It has been invigorating for us both. I'm sure that you are aware of how your books help to change lives, a little feedback can't help but reassure that the seeds you have provided are finding soil in this new Christian heart.

-Alan

"The MAL study is going great! Our Sunday School has grown 20 percent since we started, and the Sunday we shared LIFE we broke a record since I have been here. The people are really loving it, especially the teachers. I am really promoting it from the pulpit and have started putting pillars, one representing each area of the Christian life, in the sanctuary as a visual. One of my teachers, who is normally very critical of typos, told me he could not put it down. He is 5-6 weeks ahead in the study. Thanks for sharing this study with us."

-God Bless, Al

"Our church, S. H. B. C., in Alabama, has been doing your study. Each morning my wife and I do our daily lesson, and it not only brings us closer to our walk with GOD but also with each other. I struggle with faith in my life and giving it all to Jesus, but with your book, I can tell that God is working in my life and truly want to be walking in his light daily."

-Thanks, Kirk

If you have a unique experience while you are going through the book, e-mail the author at <u>Lawrence.phipps@itslifeministry.com</u>. We will only include in future editions with your permission.

Week 1

Get a

Good

Start!

DAY 1
How do I get started?

Jesus said to His disciples, "I have come that they may have life, and that they may have it more abundantly." (John 10:10; NKJ) Jesus' words in John 10:10 are the inspiration for the title of this book. Jesus wants believers (Christians) to have a life that brings us closer to Him everyday.

Mark 16:9 says, "He (Jesus) rose early on the first day of the week." This verse explains why it is suggested that the More Abundant LIFE (MAL) journey begin on Sunday. Sunday is the first day of the week. Today represents the first day of your first full week in your new walk with Christ. Take a moment to write today's date in the space provided above. Rejoice! You have taken your first step to a more abundant life in Christ.

MAL is not just a book to read; it is a walk to experience. This walk is designed for the reader to grow one step at a time toward a balanced Christian life. It is not designed to be the end of all you know, but to provide a basis for all that you will learn as a believer.

Four groups will be reading MAL. One group will be those who have recently invited Christ into their lives. Another group consists of those who are deciding whether they want Christ in their lives. Our prayer is that all will, in the early stages of reading MAL, discover what it means to become a Christian and take the step toward Christ.

The largest group who will go through this book will be believers who were never discipled. Many have become frustrated trying to build a Christian life without the proper support. If a building is constructed on weak columns, the building will crumble. If one tries to build a tall building with a narrow base, the building will fall over. Many believers wonder why their Christian lives are crumbling or toppling over. The answer can be found in the strength and size of the basic spiritual supports they have put in place.

The fourth group who will read this book consists of mature believers who have found the ingredients for spiritual success and want a road map to help others. MAL is such a road map. By reading and working through this book, mature believers will understand the principles of fulfilling the "Great Commission" of Jesus when He said to "make disciples." (Matthew 28:19) All believers will, by completing this one hundred day walk, be prepared to walk with others as they become growing disciples. Books for you to use to disciple others are available by clicking on "Bookstore" at ItsLifeMinistry.com. The first few days of MAL will help Christians insure that they have the right foundation. A verse in the Bible, spoken by a man named Paul, says, "For no other foundation can anyone lay than that which is laid, which is Jesus Christ." (1 Corinthians 3:11; NKJ) Jesus is the foundation of our lives and walk. He is as strong, deep and wide as we will ever need a foundation to be. It is a pity that so many Christians have chosen to build such weak lives on such a mighty foundation.

A 1998 magazine article from the *MAL* author stated that everything believers learn fits into seven areas of their Christian lives. I called these "seven spiritual pillars." If we recognize and strengthen these seven pillars, then we can build strong, balanced Christian lives. These seven pillars are 1. Prayer, 2. Worship, 3. Witness, 4. Bible study, 5. Discipleship, 6. Fellowship, and 7. Service. As you go through the book, you will learn about each of these.

Christians know that our foundation is strong. We must be certain that the pillars are also strong and are in place. The first seven weeks will focus on the pillars in no particular order. The pillar for each day will be identified. These weeks will provide basic biblical guidance that will help any believer get started. The final seven weeks focus on a pillar each week. They are designed to take believers to a new level in their walk and prepare them for the future levels of growth in the Christian faith.

Tools you will need

Four simple items will help you walk through More Abundant LIFE. The first tool is this book. The second, and most important tool, is the Bible. The best Bible for you may be the simplest. A hardback Bible with thicker pages is usually the least expensive and easiest in which to write notes. It is not suggested at this time to invest in an expensive study Bible with extensive comments. Select a Bible that is easy to read. Some suggestions are the New King James Version (NKJ), New International Version (NIV) or the New Broadman-Holman Bible (NBHB). Having a Bible that is easy to understand will help you commit to discover what the Bible says before you read what others say about the Bible. The Bible is the best commentary on itself.

Your third tool is a pen or pencil. Attach it to your book or Bible. Keep all three together. I-Pads and smart phones have Bible aps, but it is difficult to make notes and retain what you are learning by leaning on easy technology.

The fourth tool is time. Make time to read each day of teaching and scripture and write in each day's journal. With these four tools in hand, plus a teachable spirit and access to God through prayer, you have all you need to grow.

Your Daily Walk©

The daily devotional is entitled "Your Daily Walk"©. This concept for a daily inductive discipleship guide was developed by the author for LifeWay Christian Resources in the 2002 book Praying in FAITH.[1] "Your Daily Walk"© is divided into three sections. The first leads one to read from the Bible and record responses to questions. The second asks questions that reinforce the material studied for that day. The third section allows to reader to keep a journal of spiritual growth. When these 100 days are completed, the reader will be amazed at the progress he or she has made when early journal entries are reviewed. Remember, the early days are going to be extremely elementary. While the simple explanations may bore some, they will launch others into an abundant life from which they will never return.

Today's scripture: 2 Timothy 2:15

There are sixty-six books in the Bible; thirty-nine are in what is called the Old Testament and twenty-seven in the New Testament. Locate the table of contents in your Bible. It can be found in the first pages of your Bible. The book 2 Timothy (also written as II Timothy) is the fifty-fifth book in the Bible and the sixteenth book in the New Testament. In my Bible, 2 Timothy begins on page 1049. On what page does it begin in your Bible? _____. Turn to that page. Locate the big bold numbers on that page. These are chapter numbers. Under each bold number are smaller numbers. These are verses. It has not occurred to most mature believers that new believers need to know what chapters and verses are. Most published materials for new believers assume a great deal of knowledge. MAL does not. It may be that many Churches are not reaching the absolutely unchurched because no one is telling them how or what they need.

Notice that the first chapter of 2 Timothy has eighteen verses. The second chapter has twenty-six verses. Look at verse 15. The NIV says: *"Do your best to present yourself to God as one approved, a workman who does not need to be ashamed and who correctly handles the word of truth."* Write what your Bible says in this space: "_____

_____."

The way to correctly follow the truth of the Bible is to know the Bible. It is the author's hope that the reader's journey through *MAL* will guide him or her to know the Bible so that he or she will become a Christian who is excited about how much he or she knows.

Your Daily Walk

Review:

•To what does the writer compare the Christian life on page 8? A b_____. Growing as a Christian is much like constructing a building.

•Who is the foundation of our Christian life? (page 8) J_____. There can be no other foundation but Jesus.

•What are the seven pillars for building a balanced Christian life that are listed on page 9? 1. P_____, 2. W_____, 3. W_____, 4. B_____ study, 5. D_____, 6. F_____, and 7. S_____.

•What tools are necessary for completing *MAL*? (p. 9) (1) The book, M_____ A_____ *LIFE*; (2) A B_____; (3) A P_____ or p_____; and (4)T_____.

Journal: As you begin this walk, write below what you want God to do in these one hundred days. Your thoughts may be few or many. Do not feel obligated to fill all the space or be limited by the space if you want to write more. _____

_____

_____

_____

_____

_____

Congratulations! You have completed your first daily walk to a more abundant life. You have also written to God your first prayer of this study. May He bless you until you return to your priority time with Him tomorrow.

Make and Keep Your Appointment

Week 1, Day 2 - Monday - Date: _____/_____/_____

Appointments drive our busy lives. Some appointments get us up before sunrise or cause us to silence the phone. Some lead us to put out the *Do not disturb* sign or even miss a meal. Write in the blank your most important appointment today. _____

_____

Have you considered having an appointment with God? Suppose such an appointment were on your calendar. On a scale of 1-10 (1=not important at all; 10=the most important), how would you rate the importance of an appointment with God? _____. Most of us would say that an appointment with the creator of the universe is our most important appointment of every day. Unfortunately, many people act as if this appointment is optional. They believe it can be moved, shortened or even deleted without consequence. One of the first symptoms of a crumbling Christian life is cancelling an appointment with God. By making and keeping your appointment with Him during these one hundred days, you will begin to grow as a Christian, and your life will become a positive witness to other believers.

Set aside a time with God everyday. A daily time with God is essential to completing *MAL* and experiencing the growth that I previously talked about. You may have heard others refer to this daily time with God as a "quiet time." I call this daily time "**priority time.**" As I have grown as a Christian, I have discovered that my time with God is not always quiet and cannot always be observed in a quiet place. Even if it is not quiet, it should be priority time.

You will need to set aside approximately thirty minutes a day for your **priority time** with God. For some, their priority time will be thirty minutes before anyone else in the home is awake. Others choose to set aside thirty minutes during their lunch hour. Still others set aside thirty minutes after dinner. The earlier in the day that you have your priority time with God, the more of your day His word will be able to influence.

Let's do a five-day experiment. Look at your calendar. Set your priority time for the next five days. If you are not traveling, decide on a place where you want to do your *MAL* study. When you finish today's study, put your four tools there, and then work to return to that place during your priority time for the next five days. The last day of this week will give you an opportunity to evaluate the time and place you have set and make adjustments if necessary. You will discover in a few weeks that you will always face challenges in keeping an appointment with God. There will never be a perfectly convenient time. However, there will be an optimum time. I want to help you find that time.

Finding Your Way Through the Bible

Yesterday I helped those who are unfamiliar with the Bible find their way to an important verse. As you grow as a Christian, it will be increasingly important to easily find your way through the Bible. Many people never master this step and, to save embarrassment, they leave their Bibles at home instead of taking them to Bible study classes or worship.

Open your Bible to the table of contents. Set a goal to memorize these books. The pages at the end of *MAL* have cut-outs for the sixty-six books of the Bible. Remove, separate, put these cards in order, and hold them together with a large paper clip. The number on the back will help you keep these in order and help you check yourself as you begin to learn them. In the blank underneath the number, write the page number of the location in your Bible where each book begins. Turning to these pages and placing the numbers on the cards will be a first step in knowing the books.

Next, detach the scripture cards. Cut along the dotted line. You will need two large paper clips. Place all the cards behind the card that says "To Learn". As you detach and begin to memorize each, form a second group known as "Working to Memorize". There will be two memory selections per week. These cards can be used as flash cards for learning the books of the Bible and the memory verses.

Your Daily Walk

Today's scripture: Matthew 6:33

The first book in the New Testament is the book of Matthew. Locate Matthew, chapter 6 and verse 33. The verse will read something like this: *"Seek first the Kingdom of God and His righteousness, and all these things will be added to you."* This verse, my all-time favorite, helped me to make Jesus my priority.

Memory Flash Cards:

Go to the memory verses you have detached and separated. Remove the card that says "Matthew 6:33" from the "To Learn" group, begin reading and memorizing, and then clip it behind the "Working to Memorize" card.

Review:

• Learn how to make and keep a daily appointment with God.

• Of all the appointments you will have each day, this will be the most important.

• Your daily time with God called "P_____ T_____."

Journal: Write Matthew 6:33 below. You can copy it from your Bible or from "Your Daily Walk." _____

_____

Take time to record your thoughts and what God is teaching you._____

_____

_____

_____

_____

Prayer: Thank God for what you learned today. _____

_____

_____

_____

_____

How do I know I am Saved? Part 1
Week 1, Day 3 - Tuesday - Date: ____/____/_____

Maybe you have heard these words: "Christian," "saved," "born again," "believer" or "eternal life." The word "salvation" sums up these words and describes what a person receives who has chosen to follow Jesus, the Christ.

You are likely reading this book because you believe you are a Christian or somebody has told you that you are a Christian. Before you read an additional page in this book, I want you to be confident that if today were the last day of your life, you would spend eternity with God.

Since becoming a Christian, I have talked to tens of thousands of people about what it takes to go to heaven. Some people believe they are Christians because they were dedicated or christened as a baby. Others believe that they are Christians because their parents were Christians. Some believe that membership in a church or denomination will cause them to go to heaven. Still others have said that membership in a church or denomination plus doing good works will get them to heaven. There are those who believe that someone else can confirm them as a Christian.

People have told me that baptism saves people. Others have said everybody is going to heaven while others say no one is going there.

The twenty-first century has brought to light the mind-set of some that killing certain people guarantees them eternal life and heaven. There are those who believe that killing themselves will cause them to go to heaven.

People have told me that following a prophet, priest, preacher, philosophy, principle or path will get them to heaven, while some say that one must create his/her own path to heaven.

The ones with some knowledge of Christianity will often say that believing in God is important. When questioned further, many are not sure what that means. Then sadly, there are those who believe that something in their past precludes them from being able to go to heaven.

More Abundant LIFE will begin by giving you both the bad news and the good news. The bad news is that eternal life and heaven cannot be inherited, inferred, conferred, confirmed, earned, deserved, gained, gathered, bought, bartered, bargained or achieved. There is no person who can give you eternal life, make you take it, plead your case for it, or create a path for you. No person can baptize you into heaven, pray you there, pay your way there, vote you there, or sign your name in the book of life. You cannot receive eternal life because you followed a man-made prescription, a cult leader's rules or an Imam's orders. In short, we cannot gain heaven, and no one person can give eternal life to us.

The good news is that you *can* have eternal life. The path is much different from the path of world religions that are constantly trying to teach people how to earn their way to heaven. There are two verses in the book of Ephesians (the tenth book in the New Testament) that describe how one gets to heaven and how one cannot get there. Ephesians 2:8-9 says, *"For by grace you have been saved* through faith, and that not of yourselves; it is the gift of God, not of works, lest anyone should boast" (NKJ).

You will notice in these verses that eternal life (salvation) comes because of our faith (our trust in God to guide our lives and get us to heaven) and because of His grace (a love that we do not deserve). You will also notice that we are not saved because of our works. It is a gift of God.

Suppose that someone gave you a magnificent two-karat diamond ring. Because you could not imagine why someone would give you such an exquisite gift, you offered him a few dollars or offered to cut his grass or clean his house. First, the one who gave the gift would likely be offended at your meager efforts to pay for an expensive gem. Second, if he or she accepted even one penny, it would not be a gift.

God is offering you a priceless gift. Attempts to pay for it are an insult to a Holy God. A characteristic of the life of the fifteenth century theologian Martin Luther was his anger at the church for selling indulgences. The Renaissance church had convinced its members that if they gave a certain amount of money, then they would go to heaven. A man named Tetzel mocked this practice by exclaiming, "As soon as the coin in the coffer rings, the soul from purgatory springs."[2]

If we cannot earn our way to heaven, then why do Christians serve and give? The late Dr. D. James Kennedy, founding pastor of the great Coral Ridge Presbyterian Church in Fort Lauderdale, Florida, taught me that what we do as Christians is our way of saying thanks to God for the gift of eternal life that He has given to us.[3]

How do we know we have eternal life? You will read Part 2 of "Am I Really Saved?" tomorrow. Today's "Daily Walk" will help you prepare to discover the best news you will ever learn tomorrow.

Your Daily Walk

Today's scripture: Ephesians 2:8-9

Locate and underline this verse in your Bible. It is an important truth that explains the powerful gift of salvation and the marvelous love of God.

Review:
- Is there a man-made religion or path that will get you to heaven? _____
- Heaven comes because of our f_____ and God's g_____.

Journal: You may want to write some of the new insights that you have gained from today's study. Record you thoughts in the space provided: _____
_____
_____
_____
_____
_____

Prayer: _____
_____
_____

How do I know I am Saved? Part 2
Week 1, Day 4 - Wednesday - Date: _____/_____/_____

Yesterday you learned that there are many man-made ideas about how to get to heaven. Today you will learn God's specific plan for receiving eternal life and heaven. The Bible says we can **know** that we have eternal life. *"These things I have written to you who believe in the name of the Son of God, that you may **know** that you have eternal life...* (1 John 5:13; NKJ).

The word *life* is so vibrant that I had to find a way to use it to describe how a person can know that he/she is going to heaven. As a result, I wrote the book *It's* LIFE. The following acrostic is from *It's* LIFE.[4]

1.   The **L** in LIFE stands for **L**ove. God is love (1 John 4:8). The Bible says that God loved us first (1 John 4:10). He showed us this love by giving us His Son. John 3:16 says, *"For God so loved the world that He gave His only begotten Son, that whoever believes in Him should not perish but have everlasting life"* (NKJ).

God also gave us the grace to be saved. Yesterday you learned that it is *"... by grace you have been saved through faith, and that not of yourselves; it is the gift of God, not of works, lest anyone should boast"* (Ephesians 2:8-9, NKJ). These verses teach that one becomes a Christian (is *saved*) because of God's unearned love (*grace*) and a person's belief in Jesus (*faith*). We cannot be saved through our deeds, honesty, attitudes, religion or anything other than Jesus.

2.   The **I** in LIFE stands for **I**mperfect. The reason that we will not automatically go to heaven is that we are imperfect. The Bible, in Romans 3:23 says, *"For all have sinned and fall short of the glory of God"* (NKJ). Sin is disobeying God. All of us have disobeyed Him. We have all been caught and are guilty. Romans 6:23 defines the penalty when it explains that we are not allowed to live eternally with God unless we have received His gift of grace: *"For the wages of sin is death, but the gift of God is eternal life in Christ Jesus our Lord"* (Romans 6:23, NKJ). Take heart. The good news is that guilty people can be set free.

3.   The **F** in LIFE stands for **F**orgiveness. *"In Jesus we have... forgiveness..."* (Ephesians 1:7). Ask yourself the following question. Has Jesus forgiven me? He has if you understand, believe and receive the three 'Rs' of repentance.

(1) **R**ecognize that Jesus is the only way to heaven. Jesus said *"I am the way, the truth, and the life. No one comes to the Father except through Me"* (John 14:6; NKJ). Jesus came to include everyone and not exclude anyone. We were already excluded. *"For God did not send His Son into the world to condemn the world...he who does not believe is condemned already."* (John 3:17-18, NKJ).

(2) **R**esolve to follow Jesus. Salvation does not come just because of a prayer, but because we want to turn and follow Jesus. We decide to follow Him, and He directs our lives. The Bible says ,*"But sanctify* (dedicate yourself to) *the Lord God in your hearts* (spiritual life)*"* (1 Peter 3:15; NKJ).

(3) **R**epent to be included in heaven. Jesus said we cannot go to heaven unless we repent (turn) from our past and trust Him with our future. He said, *"I tell you, no; but unless you repent you will all likewise perish"* (Luke 13:3; NKJ).

4. The **E** in LIFE stands for **E**ternal life. If we follow Jesus, then God gives us eternal life with Him now and later in heaven. Jesus said, *"And I give them eternal life, and they shall never perish; neither shall anyone snatch them out of My hand"* (John 10:28; NKJ).[4]

Have you recognized, resolved and repented? The Bible says, *"That if you confess with your mouth Jesus is Lord, and believe in your heart that God has raised Him from the dead, you will be saved"* (Romans 10:9). Today could be your day of salvation. Notice LIFE in this request to God:

"Heavenly Father, I believe that you love me and gave your Son to die for me. I also know I have sinned and need to be forgiven. Lord Jesus, I want to turn from sin and my past, and ask you to forgive me. Please come into my life, be the Lord of my life, and give me eternal life. Thank-you for forgiving me, coming into my life, and giving me eternal life. Amen."

If you are not certain that you would go to heaven if you died today, you *can* be certain. Ask Jesus to save you by talking to Him. Use the words above as your guide and invite Him to come into your life.

Now, complete "Your Daily Walk" for today. If you know for certain that you are a Christian, take this moment to thank God for His love and eternal life.

Your Daily Walk

Today's scripture: John 3:16

The book of John is the fourth book in the New Testament. There are three other books in the New Testament called John; 1 John, 2 John and 3 John. Turn to John (the fourth book), Chapter 3 and verse 16. Of all the verses you read today, this is the most important. Underline this verse in your Bible.

Memory verse: Remove the card that says "John 3:16" from your "To Learn" group and move it to your "Working to Memorize" group.

Review: Complete the following from today's study:
- The L in LIFE stands for L_____.
- The I in LIFE stands for I_____.
- The F in LIFE stands for F_____.
- The E in LIFE stands for E_____ life.

Journal: •Do you know that you are saved? _____. If yes, write the year you invited Jesus into your life in this blank: _____.

•If you invited Jesus into your life today or recently, write today's date. "I invited Jesus into my life and became a Christian on _____/_____/_____."

•Do you remember whom God used to lead you to Christ? If so, write his/her/their name(s) here. _____

•Write down the events surrounding your becoming a Christian. _____

_____

_____

_____

Prayer: Take time today to thank God for sending His Son, Jesus, to save you. _____

_____

_____

I am Saved. Now What?

A timely question a new believer or a believer who has not enjoyed much spiritual growth could ask would be, "I'm saved, now what?" The Bible says, *"Therefore, if anyone is in Christ, he is a new creation; the old has gone, the new has come!"* (2 Corinthians 5:17, NIV) At Vaughn Forest Church we baptized new believers in shirts with this verse printed on the back. After baptism they kept the shirts. It was a joy to see believers running in neighborhoods and working in yards with shirts that had our logo on the front and God's word on the back. When we saw these shirts we knew that we had helped that person to find and follow Christ.

New believers are like newborn babies. Newborns must be nurtured by others to survive and thrive. Studies have proven that the better the nurturing process, the better the child does in life. Children need 1. A loving environment; 2. A proper diet; 3. Exercise; 4. Shelter; and 5. People in order to achieve their maximum potential.

New believers also need to be nurtured. The better the nurturing process, the better witness for the Kingdom of God the believer becomes. There are five important ingredients to becoming a healthy, growing, reproducing Christian:

1.   New believers need a loving environment to become all God wants them to be. Hebrews 10:25 says: *"Let us not give up meeting together, as some are in the habit of doing, but let us encourage one another"* (NIV). The church is a group of people who meet together to honor God and to teach, learn from and encourage other believers. In a real sense, the church is a family, but it is connected to many other families (churches). You need to find a church environment in which you can grow. God's design is for the Christian to grow and serve through the church.

2.   New believers need a proper diet. 1 Peter 2:2 says: *"Like newborn babies, crave pure spiritual milk, so that by it you may grow up in your salvation"* (NIV). The Bible is the best food for the new believer. Before you spend a great deal of time reading what others say about the Bible, read what the Bible says. The best place to begin reading is in the book of John. In that book you will discover more about the life and ministry of Jesus than any other book. Guides such as *More Abundant LIFE* and daily devotion guides can help you understand the Bible but are not to be read without also reading the Bible.

3.   New believers need exercise. James 1:22 says, *"Do not merely listen to the word, and so deceive yourselves. Do what it says"* (NIV). In a few days you will learn how to listen to God. Christians should not only listen, but also act on what they hear. Reading the word of God and exercising by putting what you learn into practice will help you to grow.

4.   New believers need shelter. In 2 Thessalonians 3:3, Paul says: *"But the Lord is faithful, and he will strengthen and protect you from the evil one"* (NKJ). God, through His church, also provides protection for the new believer. There are tests and trials that all believers face. The fellowship of Christians helps us

to not only survive the tough times but also grow because of them.

    5.   New believers need a loving Father. "Such confidence as this is ours through Christ before God. [5]Not that we are sufficient in ourselves to claim anything for ourselves, but our sufficiency comes from God." (2 Corinthians 3:4-5). A child needs a parent, adoptive parent or surrogate parent. As a believer, your heavenly Father will be the most loving parent you could imagine. He is all-sufficient. He will supply everything you need to grow as a Christian. Get to know Him, learn to trust Him and grow to love Him. You can depend on Him.

Your Daily Walk

Today's scripture: Ephesians 4:14-15

    The Bible teaches that God wants us to become mature. He does not want us to stay as infants. He wants us to "grow up." As you read these two verses today, remember that God wants to do everything to help you to grow in Him. Review:

    •New Christians are called new c_____.

    •What are the five important ingredients to growth for a believer?

    1. A loving e_____ 2. Proper d_____ 3. E_____

4. S_____ and 5. A loving F_____ on whom he/she can depend.

Journal:

    Record your thoughts about the past day. What is God teaching you that is helping you to grow? _____

_____

_____

_____

_____

_____

_____

_____

_____

_____

_____

Prayer: Conclude today's priority time by asking God to help you depend upon Him.

_____

_____

_____

_____

_____

_____

_____

_____

_____

_____

What Does that Mean?

Week 1, Day 6 - Friday - Date: _____/_____/_____

Terms that are simple to church members often confuse new Christians and unbelievers. Today's goal is to give an understanding of some of the language of the Church. Some reading MAL who have been Christians for a while may have experienced long-term believers assuming you knew things you did not know. You have discovered that assumption is the lowest form of knowledge. By the way, please take time to look up the verses that are listed beside the terms below.

Bible Terms

Apostle – the twelve individuals who traveled with Jesus (also called disciples), eleven of whom launched the ministry of Christianity after Jesus ascended to heaven (Matthew 10:2-4). Paul also referred to himself as an apostle who was *"born out of due time."* (1 Corinthians 15:8, NKJ)

Baptism – the act of immersing a believer in water such as the baptism of Jesus. (Matthew 3:16)

Church - the congregation of Christians (Matthew 16:18). The church is not a building but the gathering of believers for the glory of God.

Communion (or, the Lord's Supper) - from the last supper Jesus had with His disciples. The church continues to commemorate the life, death and resurrection of Jesus by breaking bread, representing the body of Christ, and giving the cup, representing the blood of Christ (Matthew 26:26-30).

Discipleship – the process of helping Christians grow in the seven pillars of our faith. A disciple of Jesus seeks to follow the teachings and instructions of Jesus (Luke 6:40). Jesus called the first disciples and then instructed them and His disciples today to make more disciples (Matthew 28:19).

Evangelism – the sharing the good news; being witnesses. Christians are called to be witnesses by telling others the good news about Jesus. Witnessing to unbelievers is called evangelism (2 Timothy 2:5; Acts 1:8).

Fellowship – to associate with, participate with, share with, have community with and minister to other believers (Acts 2:42).

Gift (or, Spiritual gift) - describes the unique way that God works through the life of a believer. For example, someone who leads the teaching of the word of God is viewed as having the gift of teaching (1 Corinthians 12:7).

Prayer - the believer's conversation with God. "Prayer is a conversation between two who love each other."[5]

Worship - the way that Christians approach and honor God. The term for worship literally means to become prostrate before the Lord. In our minds we humble ourselves and honor God when we worship. Worship is both private and public. Most of the time, worship is between the believer and God. There are regular times believers meet together and worship corporately.

Practical Terms

Bulletin – A bulletin is a guide that is provided by most churches that provides direction in worship and announcements of activities.

Prayer Meeting – When a church gathers to pray for others.

Responsive Reading – Many churches have times when the congregation reads scriptures or spiritual writings together. Generally, one person reads a sentence, and the congregation responds.

Bible Translations - Different versions of the Bible have been provided throughout the centuries to help the people of various periods in history and in different countries be able to read and understand the Bible in the language of their time. A paraphrase is a restatement of a translation. Translations return to the oldest manuscripts to interpret the Bible, while a paraphrase does not. Some versions of the Bible are:

KJV - King James Version of the Bible.

NIV - New International Version of the Bible (often used in *MAL*).

NKJ - New King James version of the Bible.

LBP - The Living Bible Paraphrase

If you see LPP, it is a paraphrase from Lawrence Phipps, author of *MAL*.

Your Daily Walk

Scripture: 1 Peter 3:15

In the NIV, 1 Peter 3:15 reads, *"But in your hearts set apart Christ as Lord. Always be prepared to give an answer to everyone who asks you to give the reason for the hope that you have. But do this with gentleness and respect."*

Review:

We learn as much about the Bible and the terms of both the Bible and the church so we can give an answer to our friends who are not Christians. God wants us to both know and tell others about what we are experiencing. The more informed we are, the better witnesses we will be.

Journal: Record your thoughts about the past day. What is happening in your life? Do you see God at work? _____

_____

_____

_____

_____

_____

Prayer: Conclude today's priority time by writing a prayer to Jesus. Thank Him for saving you and ask Him to continue giving you the courage to stand for Him.

_____

_____

_____

_____

_____

_____

_____

A Time to Reflect

You made it! You may not have believed that you could set aside a time everyday to meet with God. You have made it through the first important week of *More Abundant LIFE*. I hope that you understand why we call these daily times with God "Priority Time."

There is a time each week when disciples need to slow down, catch up and reflect on what they have learned. If you have done each day's assignment as designed, then enjoy this time of rest and review. If you missed a day or two, then return, read and recover the information that you overlooked. Each day is important. Every study is designed to build on the foundation, Jesus, and construct the seven pillars of a Christian's faith: prayer, worship, witness, Bible study, discipleship, fellowship and service.

Check your Priority Time

Today is the fifth day since you were guided to begin your priority time. How is the time working? If it is your optimum time, then stay with this time. If you need to change it, then do so, and we will guide you to check this time next Saturday.

Highlights from Week 1:

Review this past week. Record an important teaching from each day:
- Monday   - _____

- Tuesday   - _____

- Wednesday- _____

- Thursday   - _____

- Friday   - _____

Journal: Take time to write in your journal. Write down ideas and record events that are impacting your life in Christ. Record the victories and the struggles, the concepts you are learning and those you still do not understand. _____

Prayer: As you talk to God, remember to acknowledge, adore, accept, ask, admit sin, align with God, avoid the enemy, accompany God, and appreciate His blessings.
Reminder: Tomorrow is a day that believers should set aside to gather and worship God. Ask God to help you to begin today to prepare for tomorrow. Do not wait until tomorrow to rest and get ready; begin tonight.

Week 2

Learn to Talk and Listen to God

A Time for God
Week 2, Day 1 - Sunday - Date: ____/____/_____

Today is the beginning of the second week of your first one hundred days to the more abundant life that Jesus offered. Sunday has been set aside as the day of corporate worship for Christians. The Bible teaches that the resurrection of Jesus was on the first day of the week (Mark 16:9). The impact of the resurrection was so great that the first century Christians began gathering and later worshiping on the day that we call Sunday. My prayer is that you have found or will soon find a place to worship. You will learn that being with other believers is one way God will give you strength.

Last week you learned that the Bible teaches you that you can talk to God. Next week you will learn the importance of prayer. The best way that you can listen to Him today is to join together with other Christians in a place of prayer and worship. If you do not know a place you can worship, or if it is too late to find a place today, you may want to search for a church worship hour that is being broadcast by television. Whether you attend a worship hour or visit one by way of the electronic media, here are some guidelines to help you.

1. What did you notice first about the place of worship you attended, whether in person or by media? _____

_____

2. Were there words from a song or songs that expressed how you feel about God or your relationship to Him? If so, give the title or a descriptive line from the song. _____

3. Was there a part of worship that you did not understand? What was said or done that was confusing? _____

_____

4. If you know the title of the pastor's message, write it below: _____

_____

5. If you know the Bible passage he used, write it on the line below: _____

_____

6. Outline the main points of the pastor's message below:

_____

_____

_____

_____

_____

7. What did you learn that you can apply to your life?

_____

8. **Prayer**: Ask God to help you apply what you learned today to your life._____

_____

_____

_____

_____

Can I Talk to God?

What is prayer? **"Prayer is a conversation between two who love each other."** It is one part of the vertical relationship of the Christian's life. Let me analyze each part of the above definition of prayer. "Prayer is...

1. **"...a conversation...** In the first week of *MAL* a verse was used that provides a great illustration of a conversation with God. God converses with us through the Bible when He says, *"That if you confess with your mouth that Jesus is Lord, and believe in your heart that God has raised Him from the dead, you will be saved"* (Romans 10:9). We join the conversation when we hear these words from God, ask for forgiveness and invite Jesus to be the Lord of our lives.

2. **"...between two...** God is one, and you are two. Prayer is a dialogue, not a monologue nor a lecture. Always remember that prayer is conversational and personal, even when one prays in a group.

3. **"...who love each other."** God already loves you as much as is possible. The more time you spend talking and listening to Him, the more you will learn to love and trust Him.

Prayer is Simple

It is difficult to believe that the Creator of the universe cares about one person and wants to both talk and listen to him or her. God *does* care, and He is able to hear and answer every prayer.

Prayer has been compared to talking to the best, most respected friend you know. In the weeks to come, you will explore the depths of prayer as you continue through this book. To master the complex, you must first grasp the simple. Here are the "Nine A's of Prayer" from the Model Prayer. These provide a way to converse with God.

Authenticate that God is your Father - *"Our Father in Heaven...*

Adore God - *"Hallowed be Your name...* Adoration is thinking about who God is. Many Christians thank God for what He does, but forget to honor Him for *who* He is. God is the one who created all the good we see in the universe. God created you. God, through Jesus, is your Savior.

Accept God's will - *"Your Kingdom come, your will be done on earth as it is in Heaven...* God's will was perfectly followed in Heaven today. For His will to be done on earth we have to accept His will for our lives.

Ask - *"Give us this day our daily bread...* God is interested in your needs. *"Ask and it will be given to you;"* (Matthew 7:7, NKJ). It seems as though there is a special place in God's heart for new believers. Ask and take God at His word.

Admit - *"Forgive us our trespasses...* If you are asking and not receiving, be certain that there is no unconfessed sin in your life. King David, in Psalm 66:18, said that if we do not recognize that there is sin in our lives, God will not hear us. The best time to confess sin is when you know you have sinned. The book of 1 John, Chapter 1 and verse 9 says, *"If we confess our sins, He (God) is faithful and just to forgive us our sins and to cleanse us from all unrighteousness."* John is telling us to admit our sin and ask God to forgive us. When we confess, He forgives. The word "sin" comes from an archery term which means "missing the mark." There are a variety of ways that you can miss the mark. (1) You may say something you should not say. (2) You may do something you should not do. (3) You may neglect to speak a word for God when you should. (4) You might neglect doing something good for someone. (5) You could have a wrong attitude.

Align with Jesus -"...*forgive us...as we forgive those who trespass against us...* On the Cross, Jesus forgave those who killed Him and He forgave us. A sixth sin that blocks answers when we ask is to hold a grudge and not be willing to forgive someone. There is no grudge worth breaking fellowship with God.

Avoid the enemy - "...*and lead us not into temptation...* Satan is real and God is able to handle his evil.

Accompany God out of evil - "...*but deliver us from the evil one.*

Appreciate God - "*For thine is the Kingdom and the power and the glory forever, Amen.*" The final "A" is to **appreciate** what God is doing. A favorite verse of the Bible is 1 Thessalonians 5:18: "...*in everything give thanks; for this is the will of God in Christ Jesus for you.*" A truly grateful child is special to his/her parents. A grateful child of God is blessed by the Father when he/she honors Him.

Jesus' Model Prayer teaches us to pray. God will speak to your mind as you adore Him and investigate your sin. You can speak to Him as you confess sin, ask for others and yourself and appreciate His blessings.

Your Daily Walk

Today's scripture: Matthew 7:7-11

Matthew, the first book in the New Testament and the fortieth book in the Bible, has a strong word on prayer. Chapter 7, verses 7 through 11, records Jesus instructing us to ask, seek and knock. He also explains that God is a loving Father who is more interested in our needs than the best parent on earth.

Review:

•Complete this definition of prayer: "Prayer is a c_____ between t_____ who l_____ each other." (Page 25)

•List the "Nine A's of Prayer"?

1. A_____; 2. A_____; 3. A_____ His will; 4. A_____; 5. A_____; 6. A_____with God; 7. A_____ the enemy; 8. A_____ God; and 9. A_____ God. (Pages 25 & 26)

Journal: Record your thoughts about what is happening in your life? _____

_____

Prayer: Conclude today's priority time by praying and using each of the "Five A's" in your prayer. _____

_____

_____

_____

_____

Bible Study – One Way to Listen

Week 2, Day 3 - Tuesday - Date: _____/_____/_____

The Bible is the best listening tool that the believer has at his/her disposal. Day three of this week discusses getting to know God's voice by listening to Him. The majority of our educational process consists of listening. Yet in all my years in school, not one course was offered on how to listen. My goal is not to make the same mistake with *More Abundant LIFE*. Christians need to learn how to listen to God.

Listen to Paul's words to the church in Acts 20:30-32: *"Even from your own number men will arise and distort the truth in order to draw away disciples after them. So be on your guard! Remember that for three years I never stopped warning each of you night and day with tears. Now I commit you to God and to the word of His grace, which can build you up and give you an inheritance among all those who are sanctified"* (NIV). There are several reasons why it is important to listen to God by studying the Bible:

1. It is important to listen to God so that we can know what He says. There are a variety of competing philosophies and religions in this world. It is important for every believer to understand what God says so that when we hear unusual ideas, we can distinguish the truth of God from error. Religions and man-made philosophies often sound good but contradict what God says through the Bible. There is a huge difference between religions and Christianity. Religions have been formed by man in an attempt to reach God, usually by being good and doing good deeds. Christianity entered the world because God, the Father, reached down to us in the person of Jesus the Christ, His Son.

2. Second, it is important to listen to God so that we recognize when others are distorting the truth. Paul, in Acts 20:32, says that some of those who distort the truth will be other church members. No one is immune to altering the word of God to fit his/her own preconceptions. However, whenwe are confident in what God says, then we can challenge those who need to be corrected. Paul, in 2 Timothy 3:16, reminds us that knowledge of the word of God can be used to correct. Remember to always speak the truth in love, especially when correcting someone. Knowing what God says does not guarantee that you will always know when to act and what to do, but you will at least know what not to do.

3. Third, it is important to listen to God so that you can be like Jesus. Paul commended to us the word of God so that we could be built up and enjoy the blessings of the abundant life that Jesus promised in John 10:10. Study the Bible to build a relationship with God the Father, Son and Holy Spirit. Do not allow Bible study to become merely an exercise in memorizing rules. When the tough times come, the relationship will sustain you, but the rules will not.

As you study the Bible, you may find yourself puzzled like the man from Ethiopia in Acts 8:27-39. He was reading the Bible, but he could not understand what he was reading. Philip, one of Jesus' disciples, began explaining the Bible to the man, and it changed his life.

Most churches have Sunday Bible study groups. Your church may call this Sunday School, Bible Study or Life Groups. These groups, many of which meet on Sunday mornings, are led by teachers who provide a guide that members can read in their personal priority time, and then the teacher explains what members are reading when the groups meet. Be faithful in a group that can guide you through the Bible. Many of these groups will also be a great source of fellowship and relationship building. Learning God's word can be fun and should be exciting.

Week by week a Christian should grow in his/her ability to recognize the voice of God. When friends call from school, we long to be able to recognize their voices. When we talk to our spouses, it brings joy to them and to us when we recognize their voices. When our children call from out of town, we love to hear their voices. When we make business contacts, we work to learn names and voices. How much more important is it to learn to recognize the voice of God? How awesome it is when we hear God speaking to us and know it is He! The key is to listen to Him. The greatest listening tool is the Bible.

Your Daily Walk

Today's scripture: 2 Timothy 3:14-17

In verse 14, notice that Paul tells Timothy that someone else taught him. Pray that your teacher will guide you in the word. Verse 15 teaches us that learning what the Bible says helps us to become wise. Verse 16 tells us that the Bible is inspired by God and is useful for both teaching and correction.

Review: •The B_____ is the best listening tool the believer has at his disposal (p. 27). •What are the three important reasons for studying the Bible (p. 27)?

1. _____.
2. _____.
3. _____.

•A good way to get help learning the Bible is to be in a Bible study g_____.
Journal: Write the name of your church _____, and the name of your Bible study group (if you have one) _____.
If not regularly attending a study group, think of one you could join and write its name here:_____.
•**CHECKUP:** How is the *Priority Time* you chose working? Has this been a good time? If not, select another time and try it for the next week. Remember, you are looking for your "optimum time." What will be your daily *Priority Time* for next week? _____,_____. Be sure to keep this appointment. Record below what is happening in your Christian walk. _____

_____

_____

Prayer: Conclude today's priority time by asking God to send people into your life who will help you to grow to better understand the Bible. _____

_____

_____

Can I Know God?

More Abundant LIFE teaches that prayer is a conversation between two who love each other. However, it is difficult to love someone you do not know. It is easy for God to love us. First, the Bible teaches that God is love (1 John 4:8). His nature is love, and His character is to love. Second, He has known us forever. God said to Jeremiah, *"Before I formed you in the womb I knew you, before you were born I set you apart..."* (Jeremiah 1:5). God's words to Jeremiah tell us that He knew us before we were born. He knows us better than anyone does, and He loves us.

You and I, on the other hand, have not known God forever. Some who are reading this book have known God only a few weeks. The more you get to know God, the more you will love and trust Him. The questions you must ask are, "How do I get to know God, and how do I get to the place that I recognize His voice?"

My wife Karen and I were married in 1976. During the 1976 Christmas season, Karen worked at a florist. One day I called the flower shop. The voice on the phone greeted me and said, "May I help you?"

"May I speak to Karen?" I asked.

"This is she," came the reply. How embarrassing. After four months of marriage, I still could not recognize her voice. The only thing more embarrassing would be not to recognize it today. Even with two grown daughters who have similar voice quality, I still know hers. Preachers and teachers may say some things from God's word, but learn to recognize God's voice without anyone's help.

New Christians often have trouble recognizing God's voice. A new Christian should not be concerned. However, if after several years you still do not know when God is speaking to you, then you would know that you have not spent enough time with Him. I once was pastor of a member who said that the secret to praying is to pray, pray, pray. Prayer's success does not depend on following formulas, but on practice. Just Pray!

Spending time with God requires both talking and listening. My fifth grade teacher often explained this idea by saying: "Lawrence, nobody ever learned anything talking." There is a time to talk, but there is also a time to listen. If you want to get to know God, you will need to learn to do both. It occurs to me that the one who knows the most should do most of the talking. The one who knows the least should do most of the listening. Since God knows more than we do, our relationship with Him should consist of His doing most of the talking and our doing most of the listening.

The Bible, in 1 Thessalonians 5:17, says to "pray without ceasing." This biblical instruction would be impossible if prayer were defined as "talking to God." When one understands that prayer includes both talking and listening, then he/she recognizes that the Bible's directive to pray all the time can be followed.

The life of a believer should be characterized by talking to God every day, several times a day, and listening the rest of the time. The following examples

29

will help you to understand how and when you should be listening to God.

1. Someone at work or school tells a dirty joke. God tells me to walk away and not to laugh. Was I listening?

2. An automobile cut me off. God says not to shake my fist and blow my horn. Was I listening?

3. Someone wants to know why Jesus is the only way to heaven. God reminds me of John 14:6 and encourages me to share the verse with him. Did I memorize John 14:6? Do I know what it says? Did I have the courage to share the verse if I remember what Jesus said? Was I listening to God by reading and committing His word to memory?

Getting to know God's will for our lives is the key to victorious Christian living. To know His will we must get to know Him. To get to know Him, we must spend time with Him. Spending time with Him includes talking and listening.

Your Daily Walk

Today's scripture: John 10:25-30

The verses for today record a conversation between Jesus and some Jews who did not believe that He was God's Son. The key verse is 10:27. Jesus explains that His sheep (followers) listen for His voice and follow what He has to say. Decide today to get to know God so that you can recognize His voice. John 10:27 is your first memory verse for this week

Memory verse: Remove the card that says "John 10:27" from your "To Learn" group and move it to your "Working to Memorize" group.

Review:

• There are two important aspects to prayer. What are they? T_____ and L_____.

• The best way to recognize God's voice is to spend t_____ with Him.

• How often should you talk with God? ___Once a day ___Once a week ___Several times a day ___Easter and Christmas

Journal: By reading this study and reading the assigned Bible passages, you have been listening to God today. Write what God is saying to you. _____

_____

_____

_____

_____

_____

_____

Prayer: Spend a few minutes talking to Him. Record a prayer asking for help in getting to know Him. _____

_____

_____

_____

_____

Why do I Need to Talk to God?
Week 2, Day 5 - Thursday - Date: _____/_____/_____

Why pray? One could just as easily ask: "Why breathe?" The answer is that we want LIFE! You started your spiritual life by praying to the Father, asking for forgiveness, and inviting Jesus to come into your life. You became a Christian first and foremost by prayer. By developing a life of prayer, you will build on the relationship that you have begun with God. This relationship will grow in direct proportion to your prayer life.

Prayer is the first pillar of a balanced spiritual life. Prayer provides the power necessary for Christian living. You will soon learn that prayer connects all the parts of the Christian's spiritual armor and holds them in place. The most important lesson for a new Christian is to learn the importance of prayer.

Many believers want to know the secret to effective praying. The answer is to PRAY! Yesterday you were cautioned not to get so caught up in formulas, mechanics or routine that you neglect to pray. The Christian life is built on a relationship, not rules. Jesus confronted a group of people called Pharisees who memorized, followed and even created rules. His response was to tell them that they were clean on the outside but dead on the inside. Learning rules without building a relationship will create the pride of accomplishment, but not spiritual life.

The Obstacles

There are two main enemies that will keep you from praying. The first, is yourself. When you became a Christian, your character changed. Your previous life was characterized by being lost without hope and without God. Now that you are saved, you have hope, and you have God's help. However, your old character is still present. Paul, in Romans 7:18, calls this our sinful nature. He says that he has the desire to do good but cannot carry it out. You will often have the desire to pray but will be too tired or too busy to pray. You have given your life to Christ, but your old life will want to get back on the throne.

The second obstacle is the enemy, Satan (also known as the devil). Satan is the enemy of God and Christians. He is a fallen angel whose name means *liar*. He knows that prayer will give you the power to live an abundant life. He understands that prayer provides the avenue for becoming more like Christ. He knows that the more you pray, the less you will see of your old character and the more your new character will grow. Jesus calls the enemy "the thief." Jesus said: *"The thief comes only to steal and kill and destroy..."* (John 10:10, NIV). Let us break down these three parts:

"The thief comes...to steal..." God wants everyone to be saved (2 Peter 3:9). The enemy tried to steal what God wanted to give you. Prayer is the tool you used to be saved and to take what the enemy wanted to steal.

"The thief comes...to kill..." Once you are saved, the enemy wants to kill your witness. If he can keep you from praying and cause people to see your old

character more than your new Christian character, he can keep others from becoming Christians. Prayer will cause your new character to be seen more than your old one.

"*The thief comes...to destroy...*" If the enemy cannot keep you from becoming a Christian and cannot kill your witness, then he will attempt to destroy your joy. Prayer will give you joy when nothing else can. Joy is a quiet confidence that God is in control. Jesus was not always happy, but He had joy. He knew that God was in control. His prayer life was the key to His joy.

One Request

Jesus taught, healed people, raised the dead, fed thousands with a few fish and a few pieces of bread, turned water to wine and performed many miracles. If you had been one of His first followers, what would you have wanted Him to teach you to do? Luke, the second book in the New Testament, says that a follower, known as a disciple, came to Jesus, presumably representing all the disciples. Here is what was said: "*One day Jesus was praying in a certain place. When he finished, one of his disciples said to him, 'Lord, teach us to pray...'*" (Luke 11:1, NIV). Of all the requests the disciples could have made, the one recorded was the request to be taught to pray.

The early followers understood the importance of prayer. They saw the power of prayer in Jesus' life. They knew that every spiritual and physical success came after Jesus spent time in prayer. You also have a relationship with the Father. Build on that relationship. Talk and listen to God often.

Your Daily Walk

Today's scripture: Luke 11:1

Find today's verse in your Bible. Read and underline the verse.

Review:
- What is the key to effective praying? Just p_____!
- What two obstacles stand in our way? The d_____ and I. God wants you to get to know Him. Only the devil and you stand in the way.

Journal: Record your thoughts about the past day. What is happening in your life? Do you see God at work? _____

_____

_____

_____

Prayer: Take time to pray, and then record below recent answers to prayers you have lifted to God. _____

_____

_____

_____

_____

What Should I Say?

The study yesterday was designed to teach you that God wants you to know Him by spending time with Him. The next question is "About what should I pray?" The answer: "Everything!" Many Christians believe that they should not bother God with minor issues. Christians who "trouble" God with "small things," do not have as many "big issues."

The verses for Day 2 in "Your Daily Walk" are from Matthew 7. One of those verses says, *"Ask and it will be given to you; seek and you will find; knock and the door will be opened to you"* (NIV). Notice that Jesus' instruction uses three different words to tell us to pray. He said to ask, seek and knock, in other words, pray, pray, pray! The Bible also says to cast all your cares upon God because He cares for you (1 Peter 5:7).

Some years ago a pastor explained that he prays for a place to park near the stores where he shops. He explained that many Christians believe this is too unimportant. And then He said, "Those of you who think God does not care about parking spaces are driving around while I am parked!" His illustration makes an excellent point. If we are to pray without ceasing, then why would we stop praying every time we believe something is insignificant?

Step 4 of Week 2, Day 2 taught us to ask God. Whether for yourself or others, when you realize that there is a need, that is when you need to pray. People will discover that you are a Christian. Believers and unbelievers will ask you to pray for them. However, many Christians have good intentions and respond by saying that they will pray for the person but walk away and forget. Here are two important hints for praying for someone who requests prayer. First, you have the option of praying when they ask. An elderly lady approached me after a speaking engagement. She told me she was going into the hospital the next day for tests and wanted to know if I would remember to pray for her. I put my arm around her and asked if I could pray right then. Secondly, when it is difficult to stop immediately and talk to God on someone else's behalf, write down the prayer and remember to pray as soon as possible. The shortest pencil is better than the longest memory.

We also ask God for ourselves. Here are seven examples of what you can say to God about yourself. 1. Talk to God about your relationship to Him. Ask Him to help you understand and obey His word, the Bible. 2. Talk to God about your health. In Exodus 15:26, God told His people that He was the one who heals. One of God's names is *Jehovah Rapha* (the Lord who heals). Remember, He is the Great Physician. 3. Talk to God about your finances. In Psalm 50 we are reminded that God owns it all. The owner knows how to provide and to guide us to manage what He has lent to us. 4. Talk to God about your business. You will find that He is interested. 5. Talk to Him about everyday decisions such as job changes, purchases, moves, or vacations. 6. Talk to God about trials you face. Ask Him to help you overcome problems.

7. Talk to God about your family. He loves them more than you. He wants to help you be a blessing to them and them to be a blessing to you.

Do not be concerned about what to say or how to say it. Talk to God as you would talk to your best friend. After all, He is your best friend. Do not search for the right words. Just speak. He is looking at what you are thinking and feeling, not the words you are using.

Talk to God about everything. If you are having a struggle, then tell Him. He already knows, but talking to Him opens us to listening for His answer and His solution. Talk to God as soon as a problem or possibility surfaces. Talk to Him and tell Him how wonderful He is. Any time that God's wonderful attributes come to mind, stop and "adore" Him. Remember, when you are not talking to God, listen to Him. Learn to be sensitive to His voice.

Your Daily Walk

Today's scripture: Mark 11:24 - *"....whatever you ask for in prayer, believe that you have received it, and it will be yours."* When Jesus spoke these words, He was not suggesting that prayer is the avenue that helps satisfy selfish desires. He was concerned about Christians believing so that God could hear. God's goal is not to give us what our selfish heart wants, but to place unselfish wants in our hearts. Mark 11:24 is your second memory verse for this week and your fourth overall.

Memory verse: Remove the card that says "Mark 11:24" from your "To Learn" group and move it to your "Working to Memorize" group.

Review:
- What should you pray about? (Page 33) E_____!
- From Day 2, Week 1, and today, what are two ways you can pray?
1. Pray for o_____. 2. Pray for y_____.

Journal: Record your thoughts about the past day. What is happening in your life?_____

_____

Prayer: Talk to God. Ask for His help with something in each of these areas:
1. Your relationship to Him. "Lord, help me to _____
_____."

2. Your health. _____

3. Your finances._____

4. Your job or business. _____

5. Something you thought was too small to bother Him with yesterday.

_____

6. A problem or trial you are going through. _____

_____

7. Your family. _____

_____

A Time to Recover
Week 2, Day 7 - Saturday - Date: ____ / ____ / _____

You have completed the second week of *More Abundant LIFE*. How is the **Priority Time** you selected working out? If you still have not found your optimum time, then change and try another time.

Saturday is the day in *More Abundant LIFE* when disciples slow down, catch up, and reflect on what they have learned. As in week one, if you have done each day's assignment as designed, then enjoy this time of rest and review. If you missed recording an assignment, then return, read and recover the information that you overlooked. Each day is important. I pray that you are building on the foundation, Jesus, and strengthening the seven pillars of a Christian's faith.

Highlights from Week 2:
Read through each day of Week 2 and record a teaching from each day:
- Monday   - _____
_____
- Tuesday   - _____
_____
- Wednesday- _____
_____
- Thursday   - _____
_____
- Friday   - _____

Journal:
Take time to write in your journal. Write down ideas and record events that are impacting your life in Christ. Record the victories and the struggles, the concepts you are learning and those you still do not understand.

_____
_____
_____
_____
_____
_____

Prayer: As you talk to God, remember to acknowledge, adore, accept, ask, admit any sin, align with God, avoid the enemy, accompany God, and appreciate His blessings.

Reminder: Tomorrow is the traditional day to worship God. Whether your worship time is Friday night, Saturday or Sunday, ask God to help you to prepare before worship. Do not wait until your day of worship to rest and get ready. Prepare in advance so that you will get the most from worship.

Week 3

Worship, Witness, Study and Grow

A Time to Grow
Week 3, Day 1 - Sunday - Date: ____/____/_____

This Sunday begins your third week in the *More Abundant LIFE* study. Today is the traditional day of corporate worship. If you worship on a different day, then record notes from worship on this page. I pray that you have or will gather in the environment of the church to learn, grow, honor God and fellowship with other Christians. Remember, the Church is the bride of Jesus.

A great way to honor God is corporate worship. However, there are worship times available on the radio, internet and television. For the sake of your spiritual growth, let media worship be temporary and save it for times you cannot be in corporate worship, or use it to supplement your learning experience as a believer. Whether you attend worship or visit through the electronic media, responding to the following will help you to retain what you are learning.

1.　　What words from a song or songs best expressed how you feel about God or your relationship to Him? Give the title or a descriptive line from the song. _____

2.　　Was there a part of worship that you did not understand? What was said or done that was confusing? _____

3.　　If you know the title of the pastor's message, write it below:

4.　　If you know the Bible passage he used, write it on the line below:

5.　　Outline the main points of the pastor's message below:

6.　　What did you learn that you can apply to your life?

7.　　**Prayer:** Ask God to help you apply what you learned today to your life.____

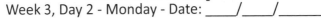

What is Worship?
Week 3, Day 2 - Monday - Date: ____/____/_____

Worship describes the way believers honor, glorify and adore God. Worship is not just gathering with other believers for an hour on Sunday mornings, nights or other times. Today we want to define worship and introduce you to both private and corporate worship.

Worship Defined

Many who read this book will know the word "worship." Some will be totally unfamiliar with the term. Many who have been Christians for years have little knowledge of the true meaning of worship.

The English word "worship" is taken from the Greek word *proskuneo* (pronounced *pros-kû-ne'o*). *Proskuneo* describes the act of a person "prostrating himself/herself before God." There have been occasions when I literally found myself face down and prostrate on the floor. However, the term is more figurative than literal. When we worship, we approach God the Father, Son and Holy Spirit. When we understand how great, powerful, loving and awesome He is, and we understand that without Him we are without help and hope, it is a humbling experience. Isaiah, one of the Old Testament writers, confronted the reality of God's majesty and thought he was dead (Isaiah 6:5). Isaiah thought that his life was over, but God lifted him up because of his humble attitude.

Private Worship

Day 4 introduced you to the "Nine A's of Prayer." The second "A" was to "Adore God." Adoring God is worship. Private worship describes every time a Christian humbles himself/herself before Go and honors God's character. There is a song that says "Holy, You are holy. Holy, You are holy. Holy, You are holy. Oh Lord, yes, You are, holy." The word "holy" means "to be set apart." The Bible says that there is none like God and no other God besides Him (2 Samuel 7:22). Singing songs like this in private worship tells God that we believe the Bible's descriptions of Him are true.

We can enjoy private worship while in our priority time, in our cars, in the outdoors, in prayer rooms and while we are run or cycle or even clean house. Anytime we can focus on God is an opportunity for private worship.

Corporate Worship

Most worship of a growing Christian will be done in private, but his/her private worship will be strengthened by regular worship with other believers. This is called corporate worship.

The book of Hebrews, Chapter 10, verse 25, tells believers to assemble together. Jesus told us that God attentively visits the group of Christians who gather according to His will (Matthew 18:20).

There are those who believe private worship can replace corporate worship. Others attend corporate worship with little or no private worship. A balanced life of worship will build both private and corporate worship.

Who do we worship?

Nothing in or on this earth is worthy of worship. No star, sun, moon or object in the sky is worthy of worship. Christians do not worship what God creates. We worship the "Creator."

Believers are often confused when they talk about God. The late, Dr. Clyde Francisco, reminded his seminary students that 1 John 5:7 says God is one in three. He used the example of water. Water can be found in various forms; liquid (water), solid (ice) or gas (steam). Each form has a unique function, but in whatever form one finds it, it is still H_2O.

God has three forms: Father (Creator); Jesus (Savior); and Holy Spirit (Empowerer). Each form has a unique function, but whatever form the Bible talks about, whether Father, Son or Spirit, He is still God.

Jesus, in His model prayer (Matthew 6:9-13), says to pray, *"Our Father in heaven. Your name is holy"* (LPP). Jesus demonstrated His love for the Father by obeying Him and worshiping Him. He spent large amounts of time talking, listening and then doing what God said.

Your Daily Walk

Today's scripture: Hebrews 10:25

Notice that the writer of Hebrews tells believers to meet together and encourage each other. Hebrews 10:25 is your first memory verse for this week.

Memory verse: Remove the card that says "Hebrews 10:25" from your "To Learn" group and move it to your "Working to Memorize" group.

Review:

- The Greek word for worship means to p_____ oneself before God (p. 39).
- Two important kinds of worship are p_____ and c_____ (p. 39).
- Whom do we worship? God the F_____, S___ and Holy S_____ (p. 40).

Journal: As you begin this week, write below what you want God to do in your life and record what happened yesterday or today that caused you to be lifted up or to need to lean on Him. Your thoughts may be few or many. Do not feel obligated to fill all the space or be limited by the space if you want to write more.

_____

_____

_____

_____

_____

_____

_____

_____

Prayer: Conclude today's priority time by worshiping God. Open your mind to Him and allow Him to fill it with the realities of His character and blessings.

_____

_____

_____

What do I do in Worship?

Yesterday we looked at why we worship and whom we are worshiping. The next question is, "What do I do when I get to a place of worship?"

Have you said or heard someone else say, "I'm going to church." Actually, we do not go to church, Christians *are* the church. We go to worship, or Sunday School or meetings. My grandmother, Mrs. Vera Phipps, would say, "It's time to go to the meeting house." The church building, house, garage, warehouse, brush arbor, or barn is only a gathering place that facilitates what happens when believers get together.

New believers are looking for worship that is alive. You may be one of those new believers. There are five prayers to help your worship be alive and vital.

1. Pray that God leads you to or makes your church a church that is sensitive to new believers or unbelievers. It may be a smaller new church or a larger new or older church. Ask God to guide you to or help your church to be interested in reaching people. You may be a believer who has searched the internet, looked for a "Church Page" in newspapers, and checked out web addresses and web sites. However, the number one response the unchurched have given for attending worship is "the invitation of a friend." Find a place you are welcomed and help your church welcome others. A welcoming church helps believers and unbelievers decide where they will go and whether they stay.

2. Pray that God leads you to a church that knows or guides your church to learn how to help guests. Look for churches that have "Guest Parking" and outside greeters. Churches looking for guests will help them get where they need to go and introduce them to a few new friends.

3. Pray that God leads you to a place that has worship guide that is helpful and informative. The guide, also called a bulletin, should give information that will provide insight into both worship and the activities of the church.

4. Pray that God leads you to a church or leads your church to leave empty seats at or near the back for guests. New attendees are often more comfortable sitting behind people than in front. Be aware there are also more distractions. As the comfort level of new attendees grows, they often move toward the front. Do not become a Christian who "homesteads" the back seats. Moving closer to the front provides guests the seats they need.

5. Grow to become an example. Participate in worship so others will also. Take your Bible, a pen and your *More Abundant LIFE* book with you so that you can read the parts of the Bible that the pastor refers to, and you can turn to the Sunday Worship day in your book to take notes.

Many new believers resist going to a place of worship because of fear, which is caused by the unknown. The above steps help reduce the unknown and reduce the fear. In 2 Timothy 1:7 we read, *"For God has not given us a spirit of fear, but of power and of love and of a sound mind"* (NKJ). God wants the unchurched to find the place where they can become Christians or worship and grow as Christians.

The unchurched and backslidden believers will talk about not coming because of "hypocrites." Isn't it interesting that we find hypocrites in every walk of life. Companies often misrepresent themselves or their products. Yet the church seems to be the only place that people avoid because of the hypocrites. Learn that the enemy, the devil, does not care if people buy food, get cable service, buy a lawn mower from, or attend ball games with hypocrites. However, he will work tirelessly to keep people from worshiping with hypocrites. An important reason we should worship with hypocrites is that they are worshiping with hyprocrites also. Namely, us! Given our best efforts, we often fail to live up to who God wants us to be in Christ Jesus. Yet we do not quit Christianity or the church. We simply seek God's forgiveness and strive to allow Christ to live more of Himself through us. We do not worship people, we worship God. He is perfect.

Many people looking for a place to worship will follow the one who led them to Christ. They will perceive that the person who shared with them is part of a church that cares about people. If that person is helping you through this book, then I double my recommendation that you attend worship and Bible study with him/her. Your growth will be accelerated because you will hear and can discuss many of the teachings within that church. Where we worship is not as important as being certain we are worshiping the true and living God somewhere. Get involved and stay involved in worship and Bible study.

Your Daily Walk

Today's scripture: John 4:23

Notice in the verse for today that God is seeking worshipers to worship Him. It is important for Christians to seek a place where they can worship Him.

Review:

- •Complete these sentences to help welcome people to worship (p. 41).
1. Pray for a church that is sensitive to n_____ believers.
2. Pray for a church that knows how to h_____ guests.
3. Try to locate a worship g_____ when you arrive.
4. You may find a place near the b_____ at first.
5. Take your B_____, a p____ and your *More Abundant LIFE* with you.

Journal:

Take time to record what steps you are taking to be more like Jesus. List answered prayers and ways that God is working in "Your Daily Walk"! _____

_____

_____

Prayer: Conclude today's priority time by asking God to lead you to the place of worship where He wants you to be at this time. If you are in such a place, then pray for those who make up the church you attend. Pray that they will be open to guests and welcome others to Bible study and worship. _____

_____

_____

How to Pass the Test

A good verse to memorize is 2 Timothy 2:15. It says, *"Study to show yourself approved unto God, a workman who is not ashamed, because he/she can correctly handle the Bible"* (LPP). There is much meaning in that verse, but the most important phrase is that first phrase. It says that we study the ible for God's approval. If we study the Bible because we want o know something, or we want to impress others, we may or may not be diligent. However, if we study the Bible to glorify God, we will likely be extremely diligent.

One day every Christian will stand before God to give account of his/her works (2 Corinthians 5:10). We will look more closely at "The Judgment" in a few weeks. For now, know that there will come a time when the works of Christians will be placed on trial. When we stand before God at the "judgment seat of Christ," there will be three important areas of accounting.

First, we must answer the question, "What gives us the right to be there?" The first week of *More Abundant LIFE* was designed to help us correctly answer the question of salvation. The only acceptable answer is Jesus! You and I can enjoy eternal life because of His life, death and resurrection and because we invited Him into our lives. Any other answer will be unacceptable.

The second area of accounting will be whom we brought with us. We will spend more time addressing our responsibility to witness in future weeks as well. Be aware that to have salvation and hoard it is selfish.

The third area of accounting is what we want to focus on today. This area is based on 2 Timothy 2:15. How much do we know? If we are to study to show ourselves approved "unto God," it stands to reason that there will come a time when He will want to know what we have learned.

Two phrases that are often used to describe what we learn from the Bible are "the milk of the word" and "the solid food of the word" (from 1 Corinthians 3:2). Paul talks about feeding the Christians milk and solid food (*"meat"* in the KJV). The milk of the word is the part of the Bible that others teach to us. Babies are fed milk. They do not eat on their own. However, babies grow up and learn to eat. Most will get to the place where they eat on their own. When they do, they graduate to solid food, just as growing Christians do.

All of the Bible can be milk, and all of it can be solid food. For example, when I was young, someone taught me about the tower of Babel (Genesis, chapter 11). I was told that the people were being disobedient by building a tower, and therefore, God gave them different languages, and the resulting confusion stopped the building of the tower. I was also taught a few things that I still cannot find in the Bible about the Tower of Babel. However, all this was milk, because someone else was teaching it to me.

Several years ago I was reading the same story in my priority time (I was "eating on my own"). As I read the first chapters of Genesis, I noticed in 1:28, *"God blessed them* (mankind)*, and God said to them, "Be fruitful and multiply; fill the earth and subdue it; have dominion over ...every living thing that moves on the earth."* God commanded mankind to spread over the entire earth. Genesis 11 records mankind's response to God. People wanted to build a city and a tower so they would not get scattered, and they could make a name for themselves. Both were against God's plan. Then I remembered that Jesus, in Matthew 28:19, told the Christians to go to the entire earth. Yet I realized that if we are not careful, we will design buildings or programs to keep our members from reaching out, and we will try to discover ways to make names for ourselves. I realized that if we are not careful, we, the twenty-first century Christians, can make the same mistakes as the first people God created.

This time the story of the city and the tower was meat. I had read it on my own, connected it to other parts of the Bible that I had read or been taught, and God helped me to make the application to my life and ministry.

One goal of *More Abundant LIFE* is to move you from relying on others to studying for yourself what the Bible says. Seek for God to teach you His word when no one else is around. Be diligent to learn so that you can gain His approval.

From milk to solid food: Genesis 11, as many teach, does not say God stopped the people from building the tower. It says in Genesis 11:8 that God stopped them from building "the city." As far as we know the tower was completed.

This information is milk. If you open your Bible to Genesis 11 to check out what I am saying, it will turn to solid food.

Your Daily Walk

Today's scripture: 2 Timothy 2:15

Memory verse: Remove the card that says "2 Timothy 2:15" from your "To Learn" group and move it to your "Working to Memorize" group. Locate and underline this verse in your Bible.

Review:

- The best reason for studying the Bible is to be _____ unto God.
- Two ways that Christians often refer to Bible study:
1. The m_____ of the word (what others teach us.)
2. Solid _____ (what we learn, with God's help, on our own).
- We can learn from others, but cannot rely on them for everything.

Journal:

Record insights and events from your growing Christian life. _____

_____

_____

Prayer: Conclude today's priority time by asking God to send someone into your life who will help you to grow and better understand the Bible. This prayer should be prayed by new believers, less mature believers and mature believers. We should never stop growing. _____

_____

_____

Our First Christian Witness - Baptism

Be excited that you are a Christian. Hold your head high and never be ashamed. Jesus said that He is ashamed of Christians who will not tell others they are Christians. Jesus came to a place in His young adult life where He let people know who He was. He did not choose to announce Himself at the Temple on worship day; He did not choose the town square on shopping day; He did not select a priest or governor to introduce Him. Jesus chose the Jordan River as the place, and He selected John the Baptizer to introduce Him. The method of introduction was to have John baptize (immerse) Him in the river.

Matthew 3:4 says, "*John's clothes were made of camel's hair, and he had a leather belt around his waist. His food was locusts and wild honey*" (NIV). John's appearance reminded people of a man called Elijah (2 Kings 1:8). John's eating habits remind us of Army Rangers who learn to survive off the land. John was telling people that Jesus was coming. Those who believed what John said about Jesus were "baptized." Therefore, he was given the name, "John the Baptizer."

The word "baptize" comes from the Greek word "*baptizo,*" which means to immerse, to submerge, to plunge. The word originally described a ship submerged under the water. A sunken ship would be described as "baptized."

When Jesus came to John the Baptist at the Jordan, He was identifying with those who had believed what John said about Him and were following John's teachings. He was also identifying with those who would follow Him in the future. John, knowing who Jesus was, did not believe that he was worthy to baptize Jesus, but Jesus insisted and was "submerged" in the water by John.

The baptism of Jesus preceded all His recorded work on earth as an adult. All evidence indicates that His preaching, teaching, healing and miracles began after His baptism. Jesus' baptism launched His earthly ministry.

Baptism is an important act of worship and witness for Christians. It can be done in an outdoor body of water or an indoor baptistry.

1.   Baptism in water is symbolic. Water represents physical cleansing. Baptism symbolizes the believer being cleansed of his/her sin after he/she has asked for forgiveness and invited Jesus into his/her life. The Bible says we are buried with Jesus through baptism and "*raised through your faith in the power of God*" to walk a new way (Colossians 2:12).

2.   Baptism is a witness. You may have been encouraged to make a "public profession" of your faith. Jesus designed baptism to be the believer's "public profession" of faith, just as Jesus was baptized to announce who He was. For this reason, every new believer is encouraged to invite family members and friends, especially non-believers, to be present when he/she is baptized.

3.   Baptism launches our ministry as Christians. When Jesus was baptized, the power of God's Spirit came on Him (Matthew 3:16) and the Father spoke (Matthew 3:17). We see a strong presence of the Father, Son, and Spirit at Jesus' baptism. In one of His last teachings, Jesus told His followers to baptize future

followers in the name of the Father, Son and Holy Spirit (Matthew 28:19).

Many who are studying MAL have been baptized. However, some were baptized before they were saved. Maybe your parents, out of love for you, brought you to God in dedication. Some have been sprinkled. However, as a believer who has made your own decision, it is time to own your baptism.

The enemy of the Christian, Satan, will do everything he can to keep you from following Jesus in believer's baptism. He will try to make you believe that believers' baptism is not important. He wants you to believe that people will think less of you and the experience will be embarrassing. On the contrary, people will think more of you and rejoice. Others will be present at your baptism who have lacked the courage to follow Christ and as a result they may be saved. I have never heard anyone, not even an atheist, make fun of another person's baptism. However, I have seen scores saved because they came to witness a baptism.

We know that Jesus submitted himself to baptism, He told us to be baptized and to baptize others, the Father and Spirit affirmed baptism, and those who have been baptized rejoice when others are baptized. Any resistance you might feel comes from an enemy who does not want you to own your baptism and make a public stand for Jesus. Baptism is the first witness that you are a follower of Christ, and it becomes your first opportunity to stand against the devil.

Your Daily Walk

Today's scripture: Matthew 3:1-17

This chapter introduces us to John the Baptist and teaches us about Jesus' baptism. Notice verse 16. It says that Jesus "went up out of the water." The only way He could have come up out of the water is to be down in the water. The name "Baptist" was given to a group of people by a group of spectators. One group was taking people into the water, immersing them and raising them out of the water. Another group was watching this practice and called these people "Baptizers." The group is now known as Baptists.

Review: •Jesus announced who He was at the J_____ River.

•Jesus selected John the B_____ to introduce Him.

•Three important truths about baptism: 1. Baptism is s_____.
2. Baptism is a w_____. 3. Baptism launches our m_____ as Christians.

Journal: When were you baptized? _____. If not baptized as a believer, talk to a spiritual leader, or e-mail me at lawrence.phipps@itslifeministry. com, and I will be glad to send you my tract on baptism. Do not delay. Call someone or e-mail me in the next day. Schedule this exciting experience for your life and future witness. •Record your thoughts about the past day. What is happening in your life? Do you see God at work? _____

_____

_____

Prayer: Conclude today's priority time by thanking Jesus for saving you and ask Him to continue to give you the courage to stand for Him. _____

_____

_____

Jesus is in the Lives of His Disciples
Week 3, Day 6 - Friday - Date: _____/_____/_____

Learn to use the word "disciple." Many like to talk about those they are mentoring. The Bible says that they are disciples. A disciple is a follower. He/She is one who is following someone to become like him/her. In some ways, a disciple is an apprentice, but not necessarily one who is learning a craft or trade.

A disciple of Jesus is a follower. Sometimes we are called believers and sometimes Christians. The word "Christian" simply means "little Christ."

You became a Christian disciple when you decided to follow Jesus, and you invited Him to come into your life. Remember that the sign of repentance is **resolving** to follow Him. The questions that many new believers ask are "How does Jesus come into my life?" and "Where does He live?"

First, look at how He comes into your life. Jesus comes into your life, when invited, through His Holy Spirit. Jesus, in John 3:8, compared the Spirit to the wind. He said: *"The wind blows wherever it pleases. You hear its sound, but you cannot tell where it comes from or where it is going. So it is with everyone born of the Spirit"* (NIV). The word for Spirit is the word "pneuma" or "breath." There are English words about breath that come from this word. He, the Holy Spirit, is described as the "Holy Breath of God." You will recall from Day 2 of this week that God is in three persons: God the Father, God the Son (Jesus) and God the Holy Spirit. These three are as one; 1 John 5:7-8 says that they perfectly agree. It is the Spirit of Jesus who lives in us.

Second, notice where He lives. The apostle Paul says in 1 Corinthians 6:19, *"Do you not know that your body is a temple of the Holy Spirit, who is in you, whom you have received from God?"* The Christian's body becomes the Spirit's residence. It is thrilling, challenging and convicting to know that Christ's Spirit lives in us. The Temple in the Bible is seen as a place where God dwells. His people would go there, and His priests would lead worship at the temple. Paul says that the body is the new temple where God lives. Thus we can worship God everywhere we go.

It is thrilling and humbling to know that our God is active in the world and cares enough to guide each of our lives. The God who created the universe, the world and all that is in this world wants to reside in us.

It is challenging because we know God gives us His power to stand and serve, not sit and soak. Jesus says: "My Spirit will give you power!" The word "power" comes from a Greek word "dunameis" where we get our word "dynamite." He gives us power when He tells us "to be witnesses." It is challenging when the Christian learns that he or she has been given power and a position in God's kingdom work to discover his or her possibilities.

However, the Spirit is also a convicting Spirit. The purpose of inviting Jesus into our lives is so He can save us and change us. We soon discover that He changes us from the inside out. He changes our thoughts, our emotions and our plans. Many try to change before they invite Jesus into their lives. They are frustrated to find they could not maintain the change. Once they invite Jesus into their lives they, too, will discover that they have the power inside of them to change. The same power that changes believers will both convict when they do something wrong and encourage when they do what is right. It is God's Holy Spirit who is using His power to change us. Sensing when we are wrong and being blessed when we are right helps us to know that Christ, through His Holy Spirit, really is in us.

Your Daily Walk

Scripture: 1 Corinthians 6:17-20

Turn in your Bible to 1 Corinthians 6:17-20. Read this passage to know what is happening in your life.

Review:

•Who lives in you? The Holy S_____ of J_____.

•What does Paul say that our bodies represent? The T_____ of the Holy Spirit.

•What does Jesus say the Spirit will give us? P_____!

•The word "power" comes from a Greek word that in English means what? D_____!

Journal: What would you like to see Christ do in your life that would make your body a better Temple? _____

_____

_____

_____

_____

_____

_____

Do you realize that what you wrote became a **prayer** to God? When you speak or write what you want God to do it is your prayer to Him.

Now record what God is doing in your life, what prayers He is answering and/or what needs you have. By writing, you will remember what God has done in your life. This is Your Daily Walk:_____

_____

_____

_____

_____

_____

_____

_____

_____

A Time to Regroup
Week 3, Day 7 - Saturday - Date: ____/____/_____

As you conclude your third week of *More Abundant LIFE*, you may need time to regroup. Do not be discouraged if you find yourself getting behind. You will discover in a few days that this is a sign that you are on the right track. If you need to change your **Priority Time**, then do so to find your optimum time.

Saturday is the day in *More Abundant LIFE* when disciples slow down, catch up, and reflect on what they have learned. As in week one, if you have done each day's assignment as designed, then enjoy this time of rest and review. If you missed recording an assignment, then return, read and recover the information that you overlooked. Each day is important. I pray that you are building on the foundation, Jesus, and strengthening the seven pillars of a Christian's faith.

Highlights from Week 3:
Read through each day of Week 3 and record a teaching from each day:
- Monday - _____

- Tuesday - _____

- Wednesday- _____

- Thursday - _____

- Friday - _____

Journal:
Take time to write in your journal. Write down ideas and record events that are impacting your life in Christ. Record the victories and the struggles, the concepts you are learning and those you still do not understand.

_____
_____
_____
_____
_____
_____
_____

Prayer: As you talk to God, remember to **a**cknowledge, **a**dore, **a**ccept, **a**sk, **a**dmit any sin, **a**lign with God, **a**void the enemy, **a**ccompany God, and **a**ppreciate His blessings.

Reminder: Tomorrow is the traditional day to worship God. Whether your worship time is Friday night, Saturday or Sunday, ask God to help you to prepare before worship. Do not wait until your day of worship to rest and get ready. Prepare in advance so that you will get the most from worship.

Week 4

Two Keys are Fellowship and Service

A Time to Glorify
Week 4, Day 1 - Sunday - Date: _____/_____/_____

Today begins your fourth week in the *More Abundant LIFE* study. Sunday represents an opportunity for believers to come together to glorify God. Your time with God and other believers will enrich your spiritual walk. Whether you are in town or on the road, the best worship experience is live. If you could be in a worship experience, then find one on the radio, television or internet and join others to worship our God. The following will help you to grow from today's worship time.

1.　　What words from a song or songs express how you feel about God or your relationship to Him? Write down titles or even descriptive lines from the songs. _____
_____
_____

2.　　Is anything said today that you do not understand? Is there anything in today's worship that confuses you? _____
_____
_____

3.　　If you know the title of the pastor's message, write it below:
_____

4.　　If you know the Bible passage he used, write it on the line below:
_____

5.　　Outline the main points of the pastor's message below. Record other Bible verses that he may refer to:
_____
_____
_____
_____
_____
_____
_____
_____
_____
_____
_____
_____

6.　　What did you learn that you can apply to your life?
_____

7.　　**Prayer:** Ask God to help you apply to your life what you learned today. __
_____
_____
_____

What does Christ want with Me?

Week 4, Day 2 - Monday - Date: _____/_____/_____

It is easy to understand why billions of people have wanted to be followers of Jesus. It is more difficult to understand why Jesus would want us. The short explanation is "love." He loved us before we were born. He wants Christians to live in such a way that others want to follow Him. In Matthew 22:35-39 some religious people wanted to trick Jesus. He quickly turned their treachery into His teaching. *"One of them, an expert in the law, tested him with this question: 'Teacher, which is the greatest commandment in the Law?' Jesus replied: 'Love the Lord your God with all your heart and with all your soul and with all your mind. This is the first and greatest commandment. And the second is like it: Love your neighbor as yourself.'"*

Before you and I learn to do anything else, the Bible says we need to learn to love God and love others. Some years ago I was looking at a cross when I considered the vertical beam and horizontal arm. It occurred to me that the vertical beam could represent our relationship to God. We often talk about reaching up to Him and His reaching down to us. Psalm 97:9 says, *"For You, LORD, are **most high above** all the earth; You are exalted far above all gods."* This verse gives us the sense that God is above us, even though His Spirit is with us and in us. The cross helps us to visualize God's desire for us to remain in contact with Him and to put Him first (the vertical could also represent the number "1").

The horizontal arm could represent the outstretched arms of Jesus who, on the cross, reached out in love to all of us. He commanded us to reach out to love others. You and I cannot truly love others until we learn to love God. We cannot love God without loving others. In fact, 1 John 4:20 has some strong words about loving God by loving others. It says, *"If anyone says, 'I love God,' yet hates his brother, he is a liar. For anyone who does not love his brother, whom he has seen, cannot love God, whom he has not seen"* (NIV). Ouch! That hurts. We must love people in order to love God? As I look at that horizontal beam of the cross, I see Jesus telling me that He loved me enough to stretch out His arms for me. I also see my need to reach out and love others.

The goal of *More Abundant LIFE* is not to turn new believers or maturing believers into judgmental Christians. We already have enough of those. Many Christians grow just enough to be proud of their growth and condescending of others' lack of growth. If you get to that point, keep praying, keep reading and keep growing. You will grow past the judgmental phase. You will grow up to become a Christian who loves people in spite of their faults and understands that his or her best efforts compared to God's perfection are like "filthy rags" (Isaiah 64:6, KJV). Since I went through that phase almost thirty years ago (and still revisit it for brief periods during weak moments), I know what it is like. Years later I realize how immature and spiritually illiterate I was. Years from now I will look back on today and realize the same thing, but I doubt I will have to hide the sermon tapes that characterized the mean-spirited, judgmental, condescending attitude that I possessed in the early to mid 1980's.

As you grow as a Christian, you will encounter people who leave the church because the pastor is not preaching enough judgment. After reading what Jesus said on the subject (you get judged the way you judge – Matthew 7:2), I decided that if I am going to make a mistake, it will be on the side of grace, not judgment. You cannot avoid those who form a system of rules they can follow and want others, namely preachers, to constantly badger others into following their preconceptions. However, you can avoid becoming one of them. Today's study is designed to help you be careful to model only Christ-like attributes that you see in other believers.

If you have been, as I was, a self-righteous, judgmental Christian, today is a good day to change. Give grace and you get grace. Leaving the attitude of judgment is not a matter of lowering our standards, but raising our awareness of how we look to a Holy, perfect God.

What does Jesus want from you? He wants you to love. All the commandments and disciplines you learn, and all the service and resources you give will be only as effective as the love you share. "*Following these commands*," (loving God and others) Jesus said, is a prerequisite to understanding the other commands of God and all that the Prophets had to say (Matthew 22:40, LPP).

Your Daily Walk

Scripture: Matthew 22:37-40

Memory verses: Remove the card that says "Matthew 22:37-40" from your "To Learn" group and move it to your "Working to Memorize" group. Locate and underline this verse in your Bible.

Review:

Look at paragraphs two and three on page 53 and answer these questions.

•What two things can the vertical part of the cross represent? 1. Your loving r_____ to God. 2. Making God number ____ in your life.

•What two things can the horizontal bar represent? 1. Jesus reaching His arms out to love y_____. 2. You reaching out to love o_____.

Journal: Write today what God is teaching you. You may want to record what He is teaching you about loving Him and others. _____

_____

_____

_____

Prayer: Ask God to help you grow into a loving, caring Christian. _____

_____

_____

Will Others Help?

Growing as a Christian cannot be done in a vacuum. God does not call us to be spiritual hermits. The book of 1 John, Chapter 1 and verse 7 says, *"But if we walk in the light, as he is in the light, we have fellowship with one another, and the blood of Jesus, his Son, purifies us from all sin"* (NIV). Those who walk in the light want to have fellowship with each other.

The last two days we have talked about spending time growing in our Christian walk. This is called discipleship. Today, we begin to learn how to work with and relate to other people. The Bible calls this fellowship. Are you in a group of believers that wants to include others in their fellowship? Does your church and Sunday School class want to be involved in helping and encouraging new believers and maturing believers? As you have learned over the past few days, it is important to ask God to help your church and class become a group of believers who are open to others.

Several years ago, I was visiting with two other people in Birmingham, Alabama. We were knocking on doors in a neighborhood to discover whose heart God might be preparing to receive Christ as his/her Savior and Lord. A young woman answered one of the doors we knocked on. I explained that we were visiting people in the area to try to discover their religious thinking and possibly assist them in finding a faith. She had a stunned look on her face as she said, "I am a Christian, but I have been away from God. A few moments ago I was sitting in the chair praying. I said, 'God if you still care about me, please send someone to talk to me so that I can get back to where I need to be.' As I was praying," she said, "You knocked on the door."

You may know someone who is looking for a group with whom he/she can share Christian fellowship. While they are looking, be aware that God may send you to them in the same way He sent us to the young woman in the above story.

The word fellowship comes from the Greek word *"koinonia." Koinonia* describes associating with, participating with, sharing with and having community with other believers. The book of Acts talks about the early disciples continuing in the apostles' *fellowship* (Acts 2:42). In 1 Corinthians, Paul says we are called to *fellowship* with Jesus (1 Corinthians 1:9). Galatians says that James, Peter and John gave Paul and Barnabas the "right hand of *fellowship*" (Galatians 2:9). Ephesians 5:11 tells the believers not to have *fellowship* with those who work evil. In Philippians 3:10 Paul wanted to know the power of Christ by having *fellowship* with (associating with, participating in and sharing of) Christ's sufferings. The New Testament provides ample evidence of the importance of fellowship.

There is another aspect of fellowship. Paul was commending the churches in Macedonia when he told the church in Corinth how these people had given to meet their needs and provided a gift of fellowship through their ministry. They not only gave what they had, but also gave of themselves to help Paul and his companions.

Becoming a part of a community of believers will provide fellowship and fellowship opportunities. It will provide ministry and ministry opportunities. There will be times when you will share and times when you will receive. In other words, you will be loved and have opportunities to love others.

We as Christians become positive testimonies to those who are unbelievers when we act like Jesus and tell others about Jesus. Being a positive verbal and living witness brings people into the body of Christ. Ministering to other believers helps to keep them in the body of Christ.

Christians become positive testimonies to believers and unbelievers when they have fellowship with and minister to others. Fellowship encourages believers as they live, work and worship inside the church. Recognize the importance of fellowship as you grow.

Your Daily Walk

Today's scripture: 1 John 1:3-7

Review:

•When Christians are walking in the light, they are having f_____ with each other.

•What are four parts of fellowship? 1. A_____ with, 2. P_____ with, 3. S_____ with, and having C_____ with other believers.

•Two ways to pray for fellowship with others are the following:

1. For you to pray for God to send you to a f_____ group, and 2. For you to pray for God to send someone to invite you to a f_____ group.

Journal: What is God saying to you today? What is He doing in your life? _____

_____

_____

_____

_____

_____

_____

Prayer: Conclude today's priority time by praying for someone who you know has a special need. It may be physical, financial, emotional or spiritual. Praying for others is another way to build fellowship. _____

_____

_____

_____

_____

_____

_____

Family Fellowship

One aspect of fellowship is what you will experience in the family of faith, the Christian community. Another important aspect is to build fellowship within the family that God has given you on this earth. A good friend of mine grew up in a family of alcoholics in another country. A preacher literally reached into the gutter and shared Jesus with his grandfather, and his grandfather professed faith in Jesus. The grandfather then led my friend's father and other family members to the Lord. Ultimately, he led my friend to the Lord. Today this friend is an internationally known preacher. He has written books that explain how the world would come to Christ if Christians would just lead their families to Christ.

Genesis 7:1 provides a telling verse. It says, *"Then the LORD said to Noah, 'Come into the ark, you and all your household, because I have seen that you are righteous before Me in this generation'"* (NIV). Noah was the righteous one, and God gave him the responsibility of getting his entire family in the safety of the ark.

The Christian's ark is the Kingdom of God. If you are a believer, then you are safely in the Kingdom. Now it is your responsibility to be certain your family is in the Kingdom.

The first important step is to rebuild broken relationships. Many families have members who do not speak to each other or visit with one another. Most of these rifts in relationships have been caused by sin. Sin may come in the form of harsh words, false accusations, greed, theft, lies, jealousy, physical abuse, or mental abuse. Many of these sins were committed when you and/or family members were unbelievers. Regardless, these rifts need to be repaired.

The Bible provides insights into mending past hurts. First, we can go to the family member and seek reconciliation. In Matthew 5:23, Jesus told us that if we know that our brother (sister) **has something against us**, then we should go to him (her) and try to reconcile with him (her). Second, we can go to the family member and seek reconciliation. You may wonder why I repeated what I said earlier. It is because Jesus said in Matthew 18:15, that if we **have anything against our brother** we should go to him and attempt to reconcile with him. It does not matter if he has something against us or we have something against him, we are to seek reconciliation.

It is true that Jesus is talking about Christian brothers and sisters, but we can easily infer that he wants us to have the same attitude toward our earthly family. Being unwilling to reconcile with a family member or anyone else is a sign of unforgiveness. Jesus told us that if we will not forgive others, then our heavenly Father will not forgive us (Matthew 6:15).

After we rebuild broken relationships, then we can re-establish fellowship with our family members. The fellowship of Christians with their families can help to set up opportunities to represent Jesus and share their faith.

Another important aspect of family fellowship is the fellowship of the family with whom you live. I understand that there are singles who are living by themselves. Their challenge will be to reach out to parents and siblings. For families where children and one or more parents, grandparents or guardians are present in the home, the challenge is to let Christ strengthen your fellowship. I learned many years ago that the future of the church depends on the stability of the home. Associate with, participate with, share with and minister to those who live in the same house with you (build koinonia). As I grow as a Christian, I am becoming more and more aware that the home and the church are inseparable. As the home goes, so goes the church. As your home becomes stronger in the Lord, you will be contributing to the strength of the church. Be a church builder by being a Christian home builder. The best fellowship begins at home.

Find an inexpensive way to get away with your family for a brief period of time. You may want to retreat for a weekend. The purpose is to spend time with your family, pray with your family and even witness to your family. This may be a good time to take this book and read Week 1, Days 3 and 4 to them. It would be a great joy if you had an opportunity to lead one or more members to Christ on your family retreat. May God use you to bless them.

Your Daily Walk

Today's scripture: Matthew 5:23 and 18:15

Underline these scripture verses for today in your Bible.

Review:

- Family fellowship may need to begin with reconciliation.
- God has given us a unique challenge to reach our families.
- The future strength of the church will depend upon the home.

Journal: What is God saying to you today? What is He doing in your life? _____

_____
_____
_____
_____
_____
_____
_____
_____
_____

Prayer: Conclude today's priority time by praying for someone in your family that needs to experience the fellowship of Christ.

_____
_____
_____
_____
_____

Let's Exercise!

By now you have learned that two important parts of spiritual growth are eating and exercising. When we digest the word of God in our spirits, we are eating. When we apply what we learn and begin to serve. We are exercising.

Jesus made a telling statement about the type of leadership He would exhibit when He said, in Mark 10:45, *"For even the Son of Man did not come to be served, but to serve, and to give his life as a ransom for many"* (NIV). He made this statement after two of His followers, James and John, requested that they sit at His right and left hands. Sitting next to the President or a famous person is a place of honor. In this case, it would have indicated that James and John were the leaders in the kingdom work of Jesus. What they did not understand was that Jesus had left His seat at the right hand of the Father to condescend and come to earth to die. There are a few recorded times when people ministered to Jesus, yet the New Testament is filled with examples of Jesus serving others. His leadership as a servant has gained Him more followers than any person in history. Today about 1.5 billion people are following Him. Over the last 2,000 years, there have been several billion more who have followed Jesus.

Jesus led by serving. We serve to exercise our growing faith. Believers find places within the church and outside the church to be used by God as builders in the Kingdom of God. What we allow God to do through us helps us to apply what we are learning. There are many Christians who have volumes of stored up knowledge, but who do very little in and through the church. A few days ago, we talked about Christ being in us and wanting to grow us as disciples. Let me caution you. Discipleship is more than gaining biblical knowledge. When we apply that biblical knowledge to our lives, then we discover its truth and worth. When our knowledge and beliefs are tested, then we find out how secure they are.

Many believers have trouble knowing where to start serving. I often tell people about a series of sermons that I preach on spiritual gifts. In a few weeks, I will go into greater detail about spiritual gifts. The sermon series was concluding, and people were still telling me that they had not found their gift and did not know where to serve. The final point of the final message on finding your gift and serving was, "Do something!" When deciding where to serve, you are not deciding between righteousness and sin. You are deciding between the good and the best. Find something to do in or through the church. If it is not exactly what God wants, He will guide you as you serve. A driver cannot change direction with a parked car, and God cannot change the direction of a parked Christian. We must get moving, and then God will take us to where He ultimately wants us to go.

What are some possible ways new Christians can serve? They can do the following: 1. Be greeters who help people out of cars and open doors for guests; 2. Be ushers who help people find Bible study classes or seats in worship; 3. Be a volunteer for a few hours a week in the church office; 4. Type bulletins or letters for staff members; 5. Drive the bus or van; 6. Play an instrument or sing in a choir; 7. Provide refreshments for groups or events; 7. Paint; 8. Cut the grass and trim the shrubs around the church building; 9. Periodically clean up the church parking lot or collect litter from the grounds; 10. Prepare a meal for a family who has experienced a new birth, grief or illness; 11. Help set up tables and chairs for events or clean up after an event; 12. Do carpentry work; 13. Feed and assist with services to the homeless; 14. Answer phones at church or other Christian organizations; or 15. Keep guests in their homes. These are only a few of the many activities available for new believers. None of the above choices require great biblical knowledge and great growth as a disciple. All they require is an available life and a willing heart.

I was a senior in high school when I first believed that God was calling me into the ministry. I shared this with my pastor. I expected him to make me an apprentice or possibly let me preach in his place. Instead, Bro. Bill asked me to drive the bus to pick up children for church. I wondered what driving a bus and becoming a preacher had in common. However, I said "yes." It was not glorious and it was cold weather when I began driving "Old Blue." Today as I lead It's Life Ministry, I am convinced that God has moved me to where I am because I started serving somewhere and allowed Him to change my direction. I did not wait to serve until someone gave me the opportunity to preach. I started moving, and God systematically changed my direction. Each responsibility that He has given me has helped me grow a little more as I have exercised my faith by serving.

Your Daily Walk

Today's scripture: Mark 10:35-45 (Read the entire story of James and John wanting to have important positions.)

Memory verse: Remove the card that says "Mark 10:45" from your "To Learn" group and move it to your "Working to Memorize" group.

Review: •What did Jesus say that He came to do? To s_____.

•How do you and I grow as believers? We feed on the B_____ and exercise by s_____.

•Finish this statement: "You cannot change directions with a p_____ car, and God cannot change directions with a p_____ Christian."

Journal: Take time to record what steps you are taking to be more like Jesus. List answered prayers and ways that God is working in your life. What is some way that you believe you can serve God? Your area of service may be in the church or it may be outside the church. _____

_____

_____

_____

_____

Prayer: Today, ask God to help you serve Him with gladness. _____

_____

_____

Whom do I Follow?

Week 4, Day 6 - Friday - Date: _____/_____/_____

Serving is an important pillar of strength that is missing in many believers' lives. The latest research teaches us that less than 20 percent of the people in a church do over 80 percent of the work. Another 30 percent do the rest, and about 50 percent do almost nothing, attend seldom and give very little. How do you and I become vibrant servants within the body of believers?

First, we must understand that Jesus called the mature believers to "make disciples" (Matthew 28:19). There are those who should have walked or are walking with you to guide you to become what God wants you to be. He/She should have guided you to learn and apply biblical truths, taught you how to study the Bible on your own, guided you to learn how to share your faith and discipled you to serve in a particular area in the church. Discipleship is not just taught; it is caught. There should be or should have been those who are helping or helped you to catch the seven pillars of strength in your faith relationship with the Father. You should then help guide others.

Second, we must realize that we are Jesus' disciples. We need mature believers to guide us so that we can grow in our spiritual lives. We need to understand that the purpose of growth is so that someday we may be able to guide others to develop as disciples.

However, there are several obstacles to leading a new believer to become a growing, reproducing disciple. Some believers do not know what plan that they can follow to help them to grow and to help others to grow. Some mature believers are afraid that they lack the knowledge that is needed to help a new believer to grow in his/her spiritual relationship.

More Abundant LIFE was written to answer the question about a plan to follow. As I said earlier, most books that I used to disciple others always assume the new believer knows certain things about the church and the Bible. Some of the books were too trite. Others were complicated and not user-friendly. My goal was to write *More Abundant LIFE* in such a way that a mature believer can use this book as a guide to help a young believer grow in Christ. These first one hundred days are only the beginning, but the testimonies in the book demonstrate that *MAL* provides a much stronger beginning than most new believers receive.

More Abundant LIFE also addresses the lack of knowledge. Many believers have been Christians for many years and do not possess the knowledge to help someone. Many need to receive help before they can give help. My prayer is that many older, but less mature believers will follow this study and receive enough information to help them recover the basics and strengthen what they have already learned in Bible study classes and discipleship groups.

Once we understand that Jesus told His disciples to make disciples and that we as His disciples have this responsibility, then, thirdly, we need to know that God has provided leaders for His church who can help us to grow as disciples. Pastors are called by God for the purpose of overseeing the body of Christ. The

Bible calls this shepherding the flock and providing spiritual direction. One of the important reasons you were encouraged to get involved in a church was to have at your disposal the teaching and leadership of pastors and other teachers within the body of Christ who can help you to grow in discipleship.

Ultimately we must follow Jesus. Others can encourage us and help to hold us accountable, but Jesus is the one who has provided the road map. That is why, in Matthew 28:20, He says, *"Teach them to obey all that I have commanded you"* (LPP). Learn to follow Jesus and seek to follow what He has selected to help guide you to become one of those future Kingdom leaders.

Your Daily Walk

Today's scripture: Matthew 28:19-20

Review these verses today. These are not on your flash cards, but it would be helpful to commit them to memory. These verses comprise what is known as "The Great Commission" of Jesus.

Review:

- Remember that you and I are disciples.
- Remember that we are called to make disciples.
- Grow so that you can lead someone else to grow.
- Know that God has placed pastors in the body to help us to grow.

Journal: Use your journal today to record the steps you are taking to be more like Jesus. List answered prayers and ways that God is working in your life as you walk through *More Abundant LIFE.* _____

_____

_____

_____

_____

_____

_____

_____

_____

_____

_____

_____

Prayer: Conclude today's priority time by asking God to help you to grow to be the Christian that He wants you to be._____

_____

_____

_____

_____

_____

_____

_____

A Time to Rejoice
Week 4, Day 7 - Saturday - Date: ____/____/_____

Rejoice for completing your fourth week of *More Abundant LIFE*. Doing anything for twenty-eight consecutive days can create a habit. In this case, you have created the best habit possible. But even if you find yourself getting behind, be encouraged. If you are reading this, then you are still engaged in the study on some level. You have this day to slow down, catch up and reflect on what you have learned. If you have done each day's assignment as designed, then enjoy this time of rest and review. If you missed any days, then return, read and recover the information that you overlooked. Remember, each day is important and every study is designed to build on the foundation, Jesus, and construct the seven pillars of a Christian's faith.

Highlights from Week 4:

Read through each day of Week 4 and record a teaching from each day:
- Monday   - _____
- Tuesday   - _____
- Wednesday- _____
- Thursday - _____
- Friday   - _____

Journal:

Take time to write in your journal. Write down ideas and record events that are impacting your life in Christ. Record the victories and the struggles, the concepts you are learning and those you still do not understand.

_____
_____
_____
_____
_____
_____

Prayer: As you talk to God, remember to **a**cknowledge, **a**dore, **a**ccept, **a**sk, **a**dmit any sin, **a**lign with God, **a**void the enemy, **a**ccompany God, and **a**ppreciate His blessings.

Reminder: Tomorrow is the traditional day to worship God. Whether your worship time is Friday night, Saturday or Sunday, ask God to help you to prepare before worship. Do not wait until your day of worship to rest and get ready. Prepare in advance so that you will get the most from worship.

Week 5

What You Need to Know to Survive

A Time to be Glad
Week 5, Day 1 - Sunday - Date: _____/_____/_____

As you magnify the Lord today, read these words from Psalm 122:1: *"I was glad when they said to me, 'Let us go to the house of the Lord'"* (NKJ). Coming together so that we can grow as we glorify God should make our hearts glad. Your best worship experience is live. If you do not attend a worship hour, listen to one on radio, television or live streaming on the internet. Today's study will help worship be meaningful to you.

1.	What words from a song or songs express how you feel about God or your relationship to Him? Write down titles or even descriptive lines from the songs. _____

_____

_____

2.	Is anything said today that you do not understand? Is there anything in today's worship that confuses you? _____

_____

_____

3.	You may write the title of the pastor's message below:

_____

4.	Take time to record the main scripture passage on the line below:

_____

5.	Outline the main points of the pastor's message and include any other verses of scripture that he refers to:_____

_____

_____

_____

_____

_____

_____

_____

_____

_____

_____

_____

6.	What did you learn that you can apply to your life?_____

_____

_____

7.	**Prayer:** Ask God to help you apply to your life what you learned today.

_____

_____

_____

Do Christians have Trials?

James was talking to Christians when he said, *"Consider it pure joy, my brothers, whenever you face trials of many kinds"* (James 1:2 NIV). Most people do not use trials and joy in the same sentence. Some people believe that Christians do not face trials. It is a fact that you and I will face trials as we go through this Christian walk. It is important to understand why we face trials.

First, you need to know that some trials can be avoided. These trials are self-inflicted. There are times that our words or actions create trials. It amazes me to listen as people create trials and then blame God. It is a testimony to the love of God that He listens to us complain and question Him, yet He still works through our trials to create good in our Christian lives.

Second, you need to understand that God works through trials to make us more of what He wants us to be. Romans 8:28 says, *"And we know that in all things God works for the good of those who love him, who have been called according to his purpose"* (NIV). Notice that the Bible does not say that God causes everything that happens, but He does cause them to work for the good of those who love Him and are called according to His purpose.

What is the best way to respond to trials? A friend of mine, Rev. Joe Murray, taught me years ago that there is one step that creates two positive results when we go through trials. The one step is to give God thanks. Paul, in 1 Thessalonians 5:18 says, *"Give thanks in all circumstances, for this is God's will for you in Christ Jesus* (NIV). Giving thanks when things go wrong is against everything in our human nature. Yet it lines up with what James says when he tells us to consider it joy when we go through trials. Notice the preposition Paul uses. He does not say to give thanks "for" everything, but "in" everything. You and I can give God thanks in any circumstance because, as Romans 8:28 says, He is working everything (good and bad) for our good because we have a love relationship with Him.

One result that comes from giving thanks in the middle of a trial is obedience. When we do what God says, even when it does not make sense to us, then we are being obedient, and obedience opens up God's supply for us. Philippians 4:19 says, *"But my God shall supply all your need according to his riches in glory by Christ Jesus"* (KJV). God has an ample supply of whatever we need. We just need to find that supply.

A second result of giving thanks when we face trials is that others see our reaction and want to know what makes us say, "Lord, I thank you that you are working in this trial for my good. I love you, and I want to be a positive witness for you, and I want you to be my supply." Ultimately, others will come to Christ because we react in a Christ-like manner. When some people go through trials, they begin to worry, complain, question, cry and even curse. Who wants to follow that example? We are not impressed by negative reactions. When a Christian goes through a trial, he/she should act without worry, complaint or unending questions. The Christian simply thanks God for what He will do and how He will help him/her to grow in and through the trial. That is an example that others want to follow.

Yes, Christians will go through trials. You may be facing one at this moment. Did you ever consider thanking God "in" your circumstance for what He can and will do through your trial? Today is a great time to start. By the way, remember the part about most people worrying? The Bible says *"Do not worry about anything, pray about everything and thank God in advance for His answers"* (Philippians 4:6, KPP).[6] This verse in the above paraphrase was the first verse my wife Karen (then girlfriend) quoted while we were dating.

Your Daily Walk

Scripture: Philippians 4:6

My wife's paraphrase of Philippians 4:6 is your first memory verse for Week 5 and your ninth overall.

Memory verse: Remove the card that says "Philippians 4:6" from your "To Learn" group and move it to your "Working to Memorize" group.

Another good passage to refer to is James 1:2-8. James tells us not only to consider it pure joy when we go through trials, but also to ask God for wisdom if we do not understand the trial. What a concept! God can help us understand our trials.

Review:

- What is James' direction when we go through trials? Consider it j_____.
- What does Paul tells us to do in all circumstances? Give t_____.
- When we give thanks, we are being o_____.
- What are the two results of giving thanks? It gets us to God's s_____, and it helps others come to C_____.

Journal: Write today what God is teaching you. You may want to record what He is teaching you about trials. _____

_____

_____

_____

_____

_____

_____

_____

Prayer: Are you going through a trial? List it below and record a prayer of thanks for the way God is going to help you to grow through the trial. _____

_____

_____

_____

_____

_____

_____

Where do I go for Answers?

Yesterday's daily walk referred to James 1 where the Bible teaches that if we lack wisdom, we can ask of God who will give it to us in abundance. People are often described as self-made and self-supporting. The truth is that we are what we are because of God and other people. None of us is truly self-made, and all of us are interdependent on others. However, the idea that we should be self-sufficient causes us to act on our own thoughts and impulses. God has another plan. Proverbs, in the Old Testament, Chapter 3 and verses 5-6, tells us, *"Trust in the LORD with all your heart and lean not on your own understanding; in all your ways acknowledge him, and he will make your paths straight"* (NIV).

When we were unbelievers, it made sense to trust our education, intelligence, instincts, background, and others. As Christians, it makes sense to trust God. Several years ago I was struggling with a decision about going to a new place of ministry. I left one Friday to teach at a conference. Normally, the conference leaders were placed in rooms with another leader. As I drove, I asked God to give me some time alone with Him to find an answer for this decision. I arrived and discovered that the pastor friend who was going to be in the same room with me had an emergency and cancelled at the last minute. I was by myself that night. I remember seeking God for answers. I prayed until I was face down on the floor. God brought to my mind Proverbs 3:5-6. These verses were significant because there was nothing about the move that made sense. God's answer was for me to trust Him and not to trust what I knew. I made the decision to move, believing that God would use me to reach more people where I was going than where I lived at the time. I trusted in the Lord, did what did not make sense to people, and watched God do a great work.

It is easy to tell people to trust in the Lord, but how do I get specific answers for the specific circumstances of my life? The Bible provides answers for every circumstance. As Christians, we learn what the Bible says so that God can bring to our minds the answer we need when we need it. Notice the illustration above. I said that God brought Proverbs 3:5-6 to my mind. God did not audibly speak to me and disclose verses that I had never read. I knew these verses and hundreds of others. When I needed this particular answer, God did not bring another verse to mind. He brought to my mind the verses I needed and had learned.

Jesus, after His baptism, spent forty days in the desert which concluded with His being tried by the devil. Each time the devil tempted Him, Jesus responded with a verse from the Bible (from Matthew 4:1-11). 1. Jesus was hungry. Satan tempted Him to turn rocks into bread and eat. Jesus responded by quoting Deuteronomy 8:3 *"Man shall not live by bread alone."* 2. Satan took Jesus to the highest point in the Temple and used scripture to tempt Jesus saying *"Jump! For the Bible says 'He shall give His angels charge over you.'"* Again, Jesus knew that God did not write this verse for Him to jump off the temple, and He responded to

Satan by quoting Deuteronomy 6:16, *"You shall not tempt the Lord your God."* 3. Satan took Jesus to a high mountain and offered to give Him everything He could see if He would just bow down and worship him. Jesus quoted Deuteronomy 6:13 and said, *"You shall worship the Lord your God and Him only shall you serve."* Jesus had spent His life learning what His Father had said through leaders, writers, prophets and His own study of scripture. When He met specific tests, God brought to His mind the verses He needed. After Jesus used scripture to resist these tests, the devil left Jesus, and angels ministered to Jesus.

There is no substitute for reading and memorizing scripture. If we are going to get answers when we pray, we need to know the voice of God and the word of God. Now you can understand why we have verses each week for you to memorize. Each week there have been two verses or combination of verses to learn. Your first memory verse was Matthew 6:33. Your next passage is Proverbs 3:5-6.

Your Daily Walk

Scripture: Proverbs 3:5-6

Memory verses: Remove the card that says "Proverbs 3:5-6" from your "To Learn" group and move it to your "Working to Memorize" group. Turn to Proverbs 3:5-6 and underline these two verses. Proverbs is a rich book with much wisdom. Choose a thirty-one day month, read a chapter of Proverbs each day, and in one month you will have read through the entire book.

Review:

•No one is self-made or self-sufficient.

•Before we are Christians, we trust in o_____.

•As Christians, we are called to trust in the L_____.

•We know how to respond to life's circumstance by studying and memorizing His word in advance.

Journal: What is God teaching you? Is He teaching you something about trusting Him? _____

_____

_____

_____

_____

_____

_____

_____

Prayer: Are you facing a decision? List it below and record a prayer asking for God's wisdom and letting Him know that your desire is to trust Him.

_____

_____

_____

_____

_____

Will I need "Good Luck"?

What is the "chance" of that happening? Have you ever heard or used these words? Growing disciples learn that nothing happens by "chance." Everything is for a purpose and is either caused by God or allowed by God. There are no other options with an all-powerful God. In Jeremiah 29:11 we read, *"For I know the plans I have for you," declares the LORD, "plans to prosper you and not to harm you, plans to give you hope and a future"* (NIV). This verse does not leave anything to chance. It tells us that God has a plan for our lives. Our goal is to discover His plan so that we can have an abundant Christ life.

Becoming a Christian includes the decision to change our ways and our language. Before I recognized that God was in control of the world and my life, I would talk about "chance" and tell people "good luck." I now talk about opportunities and say, "May the Lord bless you." One great piece of evidence that Christ was in my life was an alteration in my vocabulary and a change in my language.

Not using words such as chance and luck seems like an insignificant detail, but as we grow, we learn that words are important. Yesterday we looked at Proverbs 3. Another verse in Proverbs that is important to remember is Proverbs 6:2 that says that we are snared by our words. It is difficult for some Christians to believe the reality that we can literally speak ourselves into problems. On the other hand, we can speak ourselves out of problems. Have you said, "I don't believe I can do this?" Most of the time when we repeat these words, we do not succeed. I remember once being on a retreat. It was early in the morning, it was cold outside, and I was tired. However, I knew I needed to go out and exercise through my morning run. As I stretched, I heard a dog bark down the road where I was going. Strange dogs are not my favorite acquaintances when I am on foot. I looked down the road, picked up a small stick and said "I can do this." I ran two miles that morning through hilly terrain and returned unscathed and in a little better physical condition. It would have been easier and less productive to have said that I could not do this. I had the choice to speak my way to success or failure. I chose the former. I chose not to be snared by my words.

Horoscopes and palm readers are another snare for believers. Some years ago a church member called me and declared that she had gone to a palm reader. I breathed deeply and worked hard not to say something that would be a snare. She began to tell me how this person predicted her future, and she was concerned. The method for convincing her that the palm reader could see into the future was to discuss things from the past that, according to the woman, no one else knew. I explained to her that the devil knows our past. He knows everything we have done. It is possible for him to reveal the past to the palm reader, but that does not equal knowing our future. This woman had created a snare for her life by stepping out of God's plan and seeking a human face who she believed could know her future.

Understand that God alone knows your future. He does not give that knowledge to anyone. He knows the plans and holds the key to those plans. Reading horoscopes, trusting in fortune cookies and listening to soothsayers are not His idea of how a Christian should conduct his/her life. There were magicians in Moses' day (Exodus 7:11) and sorcerers in Peter's day (Acts 8:9). None of these were seen as righteous, and none were controlled by God. Why would we seek after people, writings and objects that the Bible instructs us to avoid?

Our goal is to be seen as righteous. Review Matthew 6:33. We are to seek God and His righteousness. You and I do not need luck; we need the Lord. We do not need someone else to predict our future because God has already planned our future. We do not need to place our trust in horoscopes (which, by the way, has the same root as "horror" and "horrible"). We need to trust in His scripture.

Growing as a Christian disciple includes putting away the old and learning the new. You should know enough by now to trust God with your life and future. Continue to discard works and words that do not honor Him.

Your Daily Walk

Scripture: Jeremiah 29:11

Turn to Jeremiah 29:11 and underline it in your Bible. It is a verse that you will return to often to remember that God is your hope and future.

Review:

•Luck and chance are not terms that believers should use.

•Proverbs 6:2 says that we are s_____ by our words.

•If someone can tell you something about your past, does that mean he/she can predict your future? _____

•One goal of the Christian is to be seen as r_____.

Journal: Write today what God is teaching you and what He is doing in your life.____

_____
_____
_____
_____
_____
_____
_____
_____
_____
_____

Prayer: Ask God to help you put away old ways and words and continue to add actions, attitudes and words that will please Him. Record your prayer on the following lines.____

_____
_____
_____
_____
_____
_____
_____

You can Win the Battles! – Part 1
Week 5, Day 5 - Thursday - Date: _____/_____/_____

Believers have won! The victory is ours, but the battles rage on. Can we win the battles? We can win them one battle at a time. Paul introduces believers to the armor that needs to be worn in order to win the battles. Today's study is designed to be a brief introduction to the Christian's armor. In a few weeks, I will go into greater detail. Reading Ephesians 6 would, at first glance, lead the reader to conclude that the spiritual armor has six parts. Since the number "six" represents incompleteness in the Bible,[7] six parts represent an incomplete set of armor to this writer. "If seven represents perfection, there must be seven parts to the armor."[8]

Read Ephesians 6:13-17. You will discover that the armor has (1) the belt of truth, (2) the breastplate of righteousness, (3) feet fitted with the readiness that comes from the gospel of peace, (4) the shield of faith, (5) the helmet of salvation, and (6) the sword of the Spirit. Any way you add it, these equal six. Is there a seventh? YES! It comes in the next verse, Ephesians 6:18: *"And pray in the Spirit on all occasions with all kinds of prayers and requests. With this in mind, be alert and always keep on praying for all the saints."* The seventh part is (7) prayer. Where does prayer fit in as a piece of the armor?

The picture of the Roman soldier's armor shows a piece that Paul does not name, the leather straps. The leather straps held the helmet on, connected the breastplate to the back plate, secured the shoes to the feet, secured the shield to one hand, secured the sword to the other hand, and represented the belt. Prayer is the connecting strap that holds each piece of the armor in place.

Let us review each piece to clearly understand the armor's purpose.

1.   The belt of truth – Why do you think the armor begins with **truth**? Jesus said, *"I am the way and the **truth** and the life. No one comes to the Father except through me"* (John 14:6, NIV). Everything begins with truth. The believer must know the truth, receive the truth, tell the truth and share the truth. The first prayer is to ask God to help you to walk in truth so that those with whom you share believe what you say.

2.   The breastplate of righteousnessMany people have said that they would become Christians were it not for the unrighteousness of those who claim to be Christians. Righteous living insures that our relationship to the Father is where it should be and promotes a life that is a shining light. Notice the breastplate guards the heart. Pray that God will guard your heart from those sins that could cripple your witness. The best guard against committing unrighteousness is to practice righteousness.

3.   Feet fitted with the readiness that comes from the gospel of peace – Once we put on our shoes, then we are ready to go. Being ready to share the gospel is a sure sign that we are not interested in just being on the defense, but that we want to be on the offense and go into battle to tell the lost about the

Good News. Pray for a heart like Jesus. Pray for God to help you to see the lost the way He sees them, and then pray for the boldness to share with them the gospel of Jesus.

The first three parts of the spiritual armor describe the character of a Christian. If we expect God to protect us, then we need to walk in the truth, work righteousness and witness for our Savior. God's protection comes from obedience, not just knowledge and not good intentions.

Tomorrow, we will look at the final four parts of the armor that God has designed in order for us to be protected and to move forward through the battles of our lives.

Your Daily Walk

Scripture: Ephesians 6:12-18

Read this and underline each of the seven parts of the spiritual armor.

Review:

• Do Christians have battles? Y____!

• Does God have a plan for protecting us and winning the battles? Y____.

• List the first three parts of the spiritual armor:

1.   The belt of t_____.

2.   The breastplate of r_____.

3.   The shoes of the preparation of the g_____ of peace.

Journal: Write today what God is teaching you and what He is doing in your life. Did you learn something new today? Record this in your journal. _____

_____

_____

_____

_____

_____

_____

_____

Prayer: Take time to pray using the first three parts of the spiritual armor. Examples are given below of how you can pray for God to help you put on His armor.

"Father, help me to represent truth. Help me to know the truth, tell the truth, and share the truth.

"Lord, guide me to walk in and work righteousness. May my life be characterized by speaking and acting in ways that please you.

"Jesus, help me to learn how to share the good news. Teach me through *More Abundant LIFE* ways that I can be a witness for you."

(Add to this prayer whatever God is leading you to say to Him.)

_____

_____

_____

_____

You can Win the Battles! – Part 2

Week 5, Day 6 - Friday - Date: _____/_____/_____

Yesterday, you discovered the first three parts of the Christian's armor. Today's study focuses on the last four. Read Ephesians 6:12-18 as you begin.

4.   The shield of faith – Paul said, *"So then, just as you received Christ Jesus as Lord, continue to live in him, rooted and built up in him, strengthened in the faith as you were taught, and overflowing with thankfulness"* (Colossians 2:6-7, NIV). We received Christ by faith; therefore, we must continue to live by faith and look at the world and God's work with spiritual eyes. When we begin walking by sight, we let down our guard (shield), and we open ourselves to the "fiery darts" of temptation that come from what the physical eyes see. God's plan will not always make sense. God's direction may not always be apparent. However, as the missionary Patrick Overton said, "When you come to the end of all you know and step out into that great unknown, you must believe that God will either give you something to stand on, or teach you how to fly."[9]

Pray for God to help you walk by faith. Dare to pray and go outside your comfort zone into the world of faith-walking.

5.   The helmet of salvation – The prayer of salvation places Jesus as the head of our lives. Paul says that believers have the mind of Christ. It is no accident that the representative part of the armor is the "helmet." The helmet of salvation guards our minds. We have prayed and received the forgiveness of our sin. Now it is time to pray that God will give us the wisdom to know when to look away and when not to listen. Pray also for wisdom to know what we need to see and what we need to hear.

6.   The sword of the Spirit – A few days ago you learned that Jesus exemplified a prepared warrior when He answered His attacks from the devil with direct quotes from what we know as the Old Testament. Every time Satan tempted Him in the desert experience, He responded by using the sword of the Spirit, which is the word of God. Believers need to learn the lesson from the Master. Jesus did not pick up the sword of the Spirit; He carried it. Each Christian needs to carry the word in his or her heart. When confronted by the world, it is easier to stand if you have memorized at least a part of Scripture than if you simply know the Bible is there.

The prayer of wisdom is critical if you and I are to remember the proper word from the Bible, and if we are to properly interpret that word to the one to whom we are speaking. Do not be complacent in your memorization to the point that you forget that God needs to direct you day by day and moment by moment to the proper word.

7.   Prayer – To follow Paul's analogy, it was said earlier that prayer is essential to keeping all the pieces in place, because the one to whom we pray, God the Father, holds the spiritual armor in place. He provides the protection that the

armor illustrates. Prayer is what ultimately keeps us close to the Father. At the beginning of this session, we learned that the spiritual armor is not designed for us to fear the devil, but to get close to God. As we talk to God, we get to know the truth. As we listen to God, we learn to walk in righteousness. As we listen to God, we receive His word to go to our neighbor with the gospel. The more we get to know him, the more we learn to trust Him, therefore building our faith. The conversation of prayer helps the helmet of salvation become relevant. The greatest listening tool the believer has is the sword which is the word of God. You will remember that prayer involves both talking and listening.

Notice what has happened during the past two days. All seven parts of the armor of God were discussed, and all focus was on our relationship to God. One can get so caught up in the analogy of the armor that he or she actually looks for a battle. God tells us to get close to Him, and He will protect us. Understand that Satan does not want us to get close to God. Our daily walk is the greatest supernatural defense against personal attacks that we have at our disposal.

Your Daily Walk

Scripture: Ephesians 6:12-18

Return to the verses about the spiritual armor. Read them and then pray.

Review:

- List the last four parts of the Christian's armor.
4. The shield of f_____.
5. The helmet of s_____.
6. The sword of the S_____, which is the w_____ of God.
7. The connecting straps of p_____.

Journal: Write today what God is teaching you and what He is doing in your life. Did you learn something new today? Record this in your journal.

_____

_____

_____

Prayer: Take time to pray using the final four parts of the spiritual armor.

"Father, help me to walk by faith. I know that without faith I cannot please you (Hebrews 11:6).

"Lord, guide me to guard my mind. Help me to look and listen for what you want me to hear.

"Jesus teach me your word. May I learn how to apply what you have said.

"Father, guide me to pray at all times. Let my life be characterized by either talking or listening to you."

(Add to this prayer whatever God is leading you to say to Him.)

_____

_____

_____

_____

A Time to Respond
Week 5, Day 7 - Saturday - Date: ____/____/_____

Until now most of *More Abundant LIFE* has been about what you need to know. As you grow, you will need to ask what you need to do. God is speaking to you. Enjoy responding to Him.

As you conclude this fifth week of growth, take today to slow down, catch up and reflect on what they have learned. If you have done each day's assignment as designed, then enjoy this time of rest and review. If you missed any days, then return, read and recover that information that you overlooked. Remember, each day is important, and every study is designed to build on the foundation, Jesus, and strengthen the seven pillars of a Christian's faith.

Highlights from Week 5:
Read through each day of Week 5 and record a teaching from each day:
- Monday - _____

_____

- Tuesday - _____

_____

- Wednesday- _____

_____

- Thursday - _____

_____

- Friday - _____

_____

Journal:
Take time to write in your journal. Write down ideas and record events that are impacting your life in Christ. Record the victories and the struggles, the concepts you are learning and those you still do not understand.

_____

_____

_____

_____

_____

_____

_____

Prayer: As you talk to God, remember to **a**cknowledge, **a**dore, **a**ccept, **a**sk, **a**dmit any sin, **a**lign with God, **a**void the enemy, **a**ccompany God, and **a**ppreciate His blessings.

Reminder: Tomorrow is the traditional day to worship God. Whether your worship time is Friday night, Saturday or Sunday, ask God to help you to prepare before worship. Do not wait until your day of worship to rest and get ready. Prepare in advance so that you will get the most from worship.

Week 6

Prayer is Basic

A Time to Gather
Week 6, Day 1 - Sunday - Date: _____/_____/_____

Today begins your sixth week in *More Abundant LIFE*. You have learned by now that every opportunity to gather with other believers and magnify the Lord is a glorious opportunity. Remember the words of Hebrews 10:25: *"Let us not forsake assembling together as has become the habit of some."* Gather so you can grow, glorify God, and be glad.

You may be in the town where you live or in another city. Strive to find a place to worship wherever you are. If you cannot attend a worship hour, find one on the radio, television or the internet. Follow these guidelines to both aid your worship experience and help you to retain what you see and hear.

1.   What words from a song or songs express how you feel about God or your relationship to Him? Write down titles or even descriptive lines from the songs.

_____
_____
_____

2.   Is anything said today that you do not understand? Is there anything in today's worship that confuses you? _____

_____

3.   Write the title of the pastor's message below: _____

_____

4.   Record the main scripture passage on the line below:_____

_____

5.   Outline the main points of the pastor's message below and include any other verses of scripture that he refers to:_____

_____
_____
_____
_____
_____
_____
_____
_____

6.   What did you learn that you can apply to your life?_____

7.   **Prayer:** Ask God to help you apply to your life what you learned today.

_____
_____
_____
_____
_____

Will I always get Answers?

Every time we pray, God answers. However, these answers may not always come in the form that we anticipated. There are several possible ways that God can answer our prayers. First, God may say yes. When God says yes, we rejoice at His response. It might be more proper to rejoice that we are lined up with Him. The purpose of prayer is not to change God's mind but to discover His heart. When we pray and we receive what we have asked, then we know that we have discovered His heart. Every time we discover God's heart, we need to rejoice.

Jesus said in John 14:13, *"And I will do whatever you ask in my name, so that the Son may bring glory to the Father"* (NIV). When God says yes, we can be assured that we are asking in Jesus' name. Tomorrow, we will go into more detail about what it means to ask in Jesus' name.

Second, God may answer by telling us to wait. When God tells us to wait, it is for two main reasons.

1.   God may tells us to wait because we are asking with the wrong motives. The prayer may be properly directed and within God's will, but our motives will cause Him to be silent (James 4:3). As we persist in prayer (Matt. 7:7), we should search our hearts to see if there is any wickedness in us (Psalm 139:23-24), and if we are open to God's showing us the problem, then when He shows us the problem, and we change our motives, God changes the answer "yes".

2.   God will often make us wait if most of our prayer time is spent asking, and little time is spent building our relationship with the Father. If His answer is "wait" (although at the time we may not know whether it is "wait" or "no"), then we must persist in prayer, search our hearts to see if there is any wickedness in us, and open ourselves to listening to what God is saying. Here are some keys to praying persistently:

(1). Pray with the purpose of getting an answer from God.

(2). Be specific in your prayer. Pray measurable prayers. Many Christians pray such broad prayers that they are not sure whether God has answered or how He may have answered.

(3). Be open to change. If the prayer is not what God wants, but you are open for Him to change the desire of your heart, then through persistence you will get your answer.

(4). Check out your relationship with God. If God seems far away, guess who moved. Hint: It wasn't God.

(5). Be open to go. God's answer may rest in you. Prepare to go if He so directs.

(6). Recognize that you may need to call someone to get agreement. Do not call for advice; you are seeking God's advice, but sometimes you need a brother or sister who will agree with you for God to work.

7.   When you know that you are in His will and convinced of His direction, stand firm. Three times in Paul's discussion of the spiritual armor (Ephesians 6:11-18), he tells us to stand. Put on the armor and stand.

Finally, God may say "no" to our prayers. Once we have followed the plan to pray persistently, and we understand that our prayer does not match His heart, then we need to pray for Him to change the desires of our heart. If he does, then we know He was telling us "no" in response to our requests. If we continue to have these desires, then he may be telling us to "wait". Keep praying and continue to get to know your Father in heaven. He will come through with an answer.

Your Daily Walk

Scripture: John 14:13

Turn to John 14 and underline verse 13 in your Bible.

Review:

•What are three ways God can answer prayers?

1. Y_____; 2. N____; or 3. W_____.

•One of the keys to getting answers is to be p_____ in our prayers.

•What is the first key to persistent praying?

Pray with the purpose of getting an a_____ from God.

Journal: Write what God is doing in your life and how He is speaking to you.

_____

_____

_____

_____

_____

_____

_____

_____

_____

_____

_____

_____

Prayer:

Pray that God will teach you how to be persistent in your prayer life. You may want to write a prayer to God.

_____

_____

_____

_____

_____

_____

_____

Ask in Jesus' Name!

John 16:24 says that asking in Jesus' name determines whether prayers are answered. Matthew 21:22 says that belief has much to do with God's answering our prayer. What does it mean to ask in Jesus' name? John's instruction was not given so believers would repeat a phrase. He knew that to be in "Jesus' name" is to line our will up with His will. If we line up our will with His, the problem of unbelief also disappears.

Another passage that helps to explain the importance of lining ourselves up with the Lord is Psalm 37:4: "Delight yourself in the LORD, and he will give you the desires of your heart" (NIV). Pay close attention. This verse does not say that if you delight in the Lord, He will give you whatever you desire. It says that if you delight in the Lord, He will "place the right desires in your heart."

When we think God says "wait", we may not know whether He is saying "wait" or whether He is saying "no". As we continue to spend time with Him, He will reveal to us if His response is to wait. It is at this point that we may discover that He has led us to wait because of the lack of time we have spent with Him. Have you prayed for something or someone and been met with silence? What kind of growing relationship did you have when you prayed? Were you listening, and did you hear what God was saying for you to do?

There are four keys that help us know that God is listening to us and insure that we are in a position to listen to Him.

1.   Return to a growing relationship with God so that our requests match His will. We can do this by delighting in Him, which is to spend time with Him, to seek to do His will, and to strive to be and look like Jesus.

2.   As our relationship changes, then the desires in our hearts begin to change. We begin to desire what God wants.

3.   As the desires in our hearts begin to change, then our prayers begin to change. We begin to ask for that which will reflect the Father's will.

4.   As our prayers change to reflect the Father's will, then the answers change to reflect our obedience and growing relationship. The Father says yes!

Many Christians make the mistake of believing that God is not listening when they do not get the answer they want. It should be our goal to discover what God wants in our lives. Resist the temptation to treat God like a spiritual Santa Claus. The goal is not to get from Him, but to get to know Him.

An Arab king summoned his son, the prince, once a year to give him the millions he would need to live on for the next year. One year, on the day of their annual meeting, the king gave his son one-twelfth of his allowance. The son indignantly explained that he could not survive on this. The king explained to his son that when he gave him a year's worth of money, he saw him once a year. By giving him one-twelfth of the money, he expected to see him more often.

Jesus said to pray this way: "Give us this day our daily bread" (Matthew

6:11, KJV). The Father could in one day give you and me all we will ever need for the rest of our lives. If He gave us today all we will ever need, how much time would we spend with Him in the future? By teaching us to pray for our daily bread, Jesus was teaching us to spend much time with the Father. By spending more time with Him, we get to know Him better and He is pleased with us. You and I are building a relationship with the God of the universe. It is time that we take this responsibility seriously. It is not about memorizing a set of rules. Nor is it about failed attempts at manipulating an all-powerful, all-knowing God. It is about learning to love the one who first loved us.

Your Daily Walk

Scripture: John 16:24

Take time to locate John 16 and then underline verse 24 in your Bible.
Memory verse: Remove the card that says "John 16:24" from your "To Learn" group and move it to your "Working to Memorize" group.

Also, turn to Matthew 6:9-15 and read the Lord's prayer with the surrounding verses.

Review:

List the four keys to help us know that we are communicating with God:

1.   Return to a g_____ r_____ with God by s_____ time with Him, s_____ to do His will, and s_____ to be and look like Jesus.

2.   Look for changes in the d_____ of our hearts.

3.   Begin to ask for that which will reflect the Father's w_____.

4.   As our prayers change to reflect the Father's will, then the Father says y_____!

Journal: Write what God is doing in your life and how He is speaking to you.

_____

_____

_____

_____

_____

_____

_____

_____

Prayer:

Pray that God will remind you daily to come to Him so that you can build a relationship that leads you to know God's voice and leads Him to respond positively to your prayers. _____

_____

_____

_____

_____

_____

Come Clean!

Spiritual cleansing restores your relationship to God. You have already learned that to have a growing relationship, there has to be daily conversation. However, if a believer has sin that has not been confessed and from which he or she has not turned, then, as the Psalmist said, *"If I had cherished sin in my heart, the Lord would not have listened,"* (Psalms 66:18, NIV). We need to be able both to listen to God and to have Him listen to us. If our daily conversation with God is blocked, we cannot get to know Him better.

The Psalmist said: *"Create in me a clean heart, O God; and renew a right spirit within me. Cast me not away from thy presence; and take not thy holy spirit from me. Restore unto me the joy of thy salvation; and uphold me with thy free spirit. Then will I teach transgressors thy ways; and sinners shall be converted unto thee"* (Psalm 51:10-13, NKJ). Sin interferes with a Christian's communication channel to God. Restoring that relationship should be the top priority of a believer. The Bible gives some good news. *"If we confess our sins, God is faithful and just to forgive us our sins, and to cleanse us from all unrighteousness"* (1 John 1:9, KJV). God is faithful. John tells us that if we confess what we know we have done wrong, He will forgive us of those sins and cleanse us of "all unrighteousness," even the sin we did not know about.

If sin blocks a believer's communication with the Father, then he/she needs to confess the sin the moment the person realizes that he or she has sinned.

Have you considered why confession is important to God? There are many theories. It certainly is not so that God will know what we have done. He knows our heart. When we admit our sin, it demonstrates understanding, honesty, and humility. It demonstrates understanding by our acknowledging that we know what sin is. It demonstrates honesty by our openly admitting we have sinned. It demonstrates humility, because we believe there is a standard, and when we sin, we do not meet that standard.

As you consider confession, be aware of the sins you can commit: committing an act that is wrong, or saying something that is wrong.

Next, be aware of the sins that come because you omit doing something God wanted you to do, or omit speaking when God wanted you to speak.

Also, be aware of the sins from your thoughts: thinking about something that was not pure and holy, or having a bad attitude about someone.

Being aware of sin is crucial if you are to build a relationship with God by cleansing your life, so that you can talk and listen to Him.

Forgive and be Forgiven

A final area that needs attention in this session is forgiveness. Our Christian journey started with forgiveness. It started on the cross where the Lord, Jesus said *"Father, forgive them, for they do not know what they are doing"* (Luke 23:34, NIV).

Every believer has received God's forgiveness. Why is it so difficult for us to forgive?

There are believers who attend church every week, teach, visit and even sometimes preach, but who have not heard from God in years. They are people that have not been forgiven. Why? Because there is someone or several individuals that they refuse to forgive. Notice the prayer the Lord gave to us as a teaching tool. You were asked to read this prayer during your daily walk yesterday. Some call it the Lord's Prayer. A better description is the model prayer. One phrase says *"Forgive us our debts, as we also have forgiven our debtors"* (Matthew 6:12, KJV). Every time we pray this prayer, we are telling God to forgive our sins the way we forgive others. In other words, if we will not forgive others, then we do not want God to forgive us.

Of all the parts of the prayer on which Jesus could have commented, there is only one portion that gets an editorial comment. Immediately after the prayer Jesus says, *"For if ye forgive men their trespasses, your heavenly Father will also forgive you: But if ye forgive not men their trespasses, neither will your Father forgive your trespasses"* (Matthew 6:14-15, KJV).

Forgiveness is essential for a Christian to have a growing spiritual walk.

Your Daily Walk

Scripture: Psalm 51:13

Underline these verses in your Bible today

Review:

•What are different kinds of sin?

1. There are sins you can c_____.
2. There are things you may o_____.
3. There are sins from our t_____.
4. There is the sin of unf_____.

Journal: Write what God is doing in your life and how He is speaking to you.

_____
_____
_____
_____
_____
_____
_____
_____

Prayer: Pray for God's cleansing in each area of your life today.

_____
_____
_____
_____
_____
_____

Come Clean! – Part 2

Jesus told us to let our light shine before men so they would see our good works, but glorify our Father in heaven (Matthew 5:16). Christians are representatives of the light. We are not the light, but reflections of the light. The only light the moon has is what the *sun* gives it. The only light the Christian has is what the **Son** gives him/her. Positioning ourselves so that others cannot see the light is a dangerous position for the believer. Disobedience creates a human eclipse, and others cannot see the Son. Our sin can turn others away from the spiritual warmth of the Son.

Why is it dangerous for the believer not to live in righteousness? Believers have a home in Heaven. If we keep others from seeing the light, then God can, out of love for the lost, move us. There are at least four ways we can be moved.

1. A believer can lose his/her influence. Psalm 1 says that if one walks in the counsel of the unrighteous, then he/she gets to the place where he/she stands in the way of sinners, and eventually is sitting in the seat of the scornful. Christians who were once contributing saints that many respected can become scornful people who have little or no influence.

2. A believer can be moved. In 1 Corinthians 5, we have the story of an unrighteous man in the church. Paul urged the church to turn him out.

3. A believer can perish. 1 John 5 is talking about the "brothers" when it tells us that there is *"a sin that leads to death"* (1 John 5:16, NIV). What is that sin? He does not say. It likely varies from Christian to Christian. It may be any particular sin that we refuse to forsake. That is a deadly sin.

4. A believer can change. When we come to God in prayer, confess our sin and turn from our sin, then we restore the growing relationship, and we become polished reflectors of the light, Jesus.

Be willing to get alone with God and ask the tough question: "Is there any sin in my life that is keeping me from communicating with You?" It is imperative that believers turn over every sin stone. When we personally admit to God what is going on in our lives, we will be guided to forsake our sin. Today's "**Your Daily Walk**" will be an opportunity to review a number of possible sins and come clean before God. To help you be honest with your answers, choose a letter from the alphabet that only you know that represents "Yes," and one that represents "No." If you do this, no one will know your answer if they see your book tonight or in the future. Chances are that you will have several yes and several no answers.

Personal Sins

Am I willing to do anything God wants me to do? _____
Am I sinning the sin of prayerlessness? _____
Have I neglected the Word of God? _____
Am I impatient? _____   Irritable? _____   Am I offended easily? _____
Do I get angry easily? _____   Do I "blow up"? _____
Do my "hurt feelings" keep me from serving God? _____
Do I "swell up" with resentment? _____   Do I covet? _____

Have I sought material blessings more than spiritual blessings? ____
Is there anything in my life that I would not be willing to give up for Christ? ____
Do I deny myself daily to follow Jesus? ____
Have I any bad habit which I should forsake? ____
Have I asked God's help? ____
Do I have sinful pride in my heart? ____   Can I keep a secret? ____
Is my mind honest and clean in the sight of God? ____
Am I faithful to my wedding vows in deed and thought? ____
Is my home a testimony for Jesus? ____
Do I have any secret sin which I excuse but should forsake? ____
Did I meet every situation today as a Christian should? ____
Have I honestly allowed Jesus to be a witness through me today? ____
Have I worried and been anxious about things for which I had no control? ____
Do I fret? ____   Complain? ____   Am I guilty of the sin of unbelief? ____
Am I willing to ask God to help me put these personal sins out of my life? ____
  Pause and confess those personal sins keeping you from being a cleansed vessel.

Interpersonal Sins

Have I forgiven everyone? ____
Have I forgiven those who talked about me? ____
Talked about my loved ones? ____   Is all resentment out of my heart? ____
Am I willing to ask forgiveness from anyone I have wronged in any way? ____
Do I bear grudges? ____
Am I critical of others? ____
Is the reputation of another safe in my hands? ____
When I speak the truth, do I do so in love? ____
Do I become jealous when others succeed? ____
Am I dishonest with others? ____
Have I paid my debts to others as I should? ____
Am I willing to leave a wrong impression if I can do so without telling a lie? ____
Do I have anything in my possession which does not rightly belong to me? ____
Have I wronged anyone and failed to make restitution? ____
Am I willing to ask God to help me put these interpersonal sins out of my life? ____
  Pause and confess those interpersonal sins which have separated you from God.

Sins against Christ and His Church

Have I broken any promise or pledge made to God? ____   His Church? ____
Since my emergency is past, have I kept the promises I made in prayer? ____
Have I hurt someone or my church by needless talk about another's faults? ____
Do I have a right attitude toward my fellow church members? ____
Toward the leaders in the church? ____
Do I really believe in the power of God to cleanse any sinner, change any life and heal any heart? ____
Am I willing to ask God to help me put these sins against Christ and His Church out of my heart? ____
  Pause and confess those sins against Christ and His Church which are keeping you from being a cleansed vessel.

Now pause and thank God for His forgiveness. Turn to and claim 1 John 1:9.

Following = Forsaking
Week 6, Day 6 - Friday - Date: ____/____/_____

The past few days have been written to help the believer understand the importance of forsaking his/her past and moving forward toward God's future. There are many people who want to be Christians in the activity sense. They attend Bible study and worship. They give. They work. They often invite others to come. The problem is that they want their positive activities to keep them from forsaking the sin in their lives.

The Christian walk is not an experience where God holds up a scale and places our sin on one side and our righteousness on the other. If He judged us this way, then we would all be lost. We are blessed that God judges our salvation based on receiving His Son, Jesus, into our lives. As we have learned during the past six weeks, He has some high expectations for us.

Jesus said *"If anyone would come after me, he must deny himself and take up his cross daily and follow me"* (Luke 9:23, NIV). He is ready for us to get rid of our past, suppress our desires and do what He wants us to do.

We should see our Christian walk as a focused investment. Jesus said, *"The kingdom of heaven is like treasure hidden in a field. When a man found it, he hid it again, and then in his joy went and sold all he had and bought that field. 45 "Again, the kingdom of heaven is like a merchant looking for fine pearls. 46 When he found one of great value, he went away and sold everything he had and bought it. 47 "Once again, the kingdom of heaven is like a net that was let down into the lake and caught all kinds of fish. 48 When it was full, the fishermen pulled it up on the shore. Then they sat down and collected the good fish in baskets, but threw the bad away"* (Matthew 13:44-48, NIV).

Christians have discovered the precious treasure. The most precious treasure that exists is eternal life with Christ and the eternal inheritance of heaven. However, for our relationship to be all that God wants it to be, we must do whatever it takes to get the treasure and discard whatever keeps the treasure from blessing God and us. Many Christians call this "surrender." However, we are not surrendering in defeat. We are surrendering because we have discovered someone better to serve. Actually, we have invested in someone better, Jesus. As Jesus becomes the focus of our lives and walk, then all those items that seemed so important do not look as important anymore.

An acquaintance of mine owned a cable and phone company. He was wealthy, but he saw an opportunity to begin a new company. He sold his assets, invested in a little known enterprise and today enjoys the income from his only financial investment, a cell phone company. Most people thought he should hold on to all or part of his past business ventures, but he was confident that this new technology would sweep the nation. He was wrong; cell phone usage has swept the world.

Cell phone companies are lucrative companies today, but who knows what tomorrow will bring? Jesus, on the other hand, is a sure investment. Besides the blessings that He provides in this life, He gives eternal life. If people sell houses, businesses and land to invest in risky ventures, how much more should we turn from our old lives to totally invest in a no-risk venture? Review what you may be holding on to that you should forsake. Forsaking the past and the world is important if we are going to be followers who make a difference.

Your Daily Walk

Scripture: Luke 9:23

Memory verse: Remove the card that says "Luke 9:23" from your "To Learn" group and move it to your "Working to Memorize" group. Today is a great time to remind you to go through these cards everyday and even several times a day. You want these verses to be engraved in your memory.

Now turn to Luke 9:23 and underline it in your Bible.

Review:

What are the three responses in the three parables that Jesus told in Matthew 13?

1. When the man found the treasure, he s_____ all he had.
2. When the merchant found the pearl, he s_____ all he had.
3. When the great catch of fish came in, they kept the good and threw away the b_____.

Journal: Write what you would like to see God do in your life that would cause you to be a 100 percent investor in His kingdom. _____
_____
_____
_____
_____
_____
_____
_____
_____
_____
_____
_____
_____

Prayer:

Pray that God will teach you what it means to sell out to Him. _____
_____
_____
_____
_____
_____
_____

A Time to Reap
Week 6, Day 7 - Saturday - Date: _____/_____/_____

You are sowing some great seeds in your spiritual life by following the *More Abundant LIFE* study. You may believe that you are doing a great deal of work for few results. Review the first week of your journal. If you were thorough, you probably wrote down some struggles that have now disappeared. Reflect on the blessings and notice that you are reaping because you have sown.

Today is a day to slow down, catch up and reflect on what you have learned. If you have completed assignments as designed, then enjoy rest and review. If you missed any days, then return, read and recover the information that you overlooked.

Highlights from Week 6:
Read through each day of Week 6 and record a teaching from each day:

•Monday   - _____

_____

•Tuesday   - _____

_____

•Wednesday- _____

_____

•Thursday - _____

_____

•Friday   - _____

_____

Journal:
Take time to write in your journal. Write down ideas and record events that are impacting your life in Christ. Record the victories and the struggles, the concepts you are learning and those you still do not understand.

_____

_____

_____

_____

_____

_____

_____

Prayer: As you talk to God, remember to **a**cknowledge, **a**dore, **a**ccept, **a**sk, **a**dmit any sin, **a**lign with God, **a**void the enemy, **a**ccompany God, and **a**ppreciate His blessings.

Reminder: Tomorrow is the traditional day to worship God. Whether your worship time is Friday night, Saturday or Sunday, ask God to help you to prepare before worship. Do not wait until your day of worship to rest and get ready. Prepare in advance so that you will get the most from worship.

Week 7

Need Help? Look Inside!

A Time to be Grateful
Week 7, Day 1 - Sunday - Date: _____/_____/_____

Today begins your seventh week in the *More Abundant LIFE* study. When you gather for Bible study and worship next week, you will have reached the halfway point. Take every opportunity to gather with other believers and honor the Lord. If you have found a group of Christians with whom you can gather to worship, grow and glorify God; this should make you grateful.

If you are in your hometown, then make every effort to worship with your church family. If you are elsewhere, then try to find a place to worship with another church family. As always, if you cannot attend a worship hour, find one on the radio, the television, or the internet. These guidelines will aid your worship experience and help you to retain some of what you see and hear.

1.   What words from a song or songs express how you feel about God or your relationship to Him? Write down titles or even descriptive lines from the songs. _____

_____

_____

2.   Is anything said today that you do not understand? Is there anything in today's worship that confuses you? _____

_____

3.   Write the title of the pastor's message:_____

_____

4.   Record the main scripture passage on these lines: _____

_____

5.   Outline the main points of the pastor's message below and include any other verses of scripture that he refers to:_____

_____

_____

_____

_____

_____

_____

_____

6.   What did you learn that you can apply to your life?_____

_____

7.   **Prayer:** Ask God to help you apply to your life what you learned today.

_____

_____

_____

_____

_____

_____

Are there Provisions?

The first week of *More Abundant LIFE* taught that one becomes a Christian when the Holy Spirit comes to live in him/her. There aremultiple benefits that God's indwelling Spirit gives to a believer. The greatest gift is Himself. Acts 2:38 says, *"Repent and be baptized, every one of you, in the name of Jesus Christ for the forgiveness of your sins. And you will receive the gift of the Holy Spirit"* (NIV). Notice that the Holy Spirit is the gift! When we experience Him, He helps us. We change from the inside out, because He, the Holy Spirit, is in us.

The Holy Spirit brings a storehouse of provisions when He comes to live in us. First, He brings what we need to learn. Jesus, in John 14:26 says, *"But the Counselor, the Holy Spirit, whom the Father will send in my name, will teach you all things and will remind you of everything I have said to you"* (NIV). Preachers and teachers talk, but the Holy Spirit teaches. It is important for us to have clean lives and receptive minds so we can learn. It is important for those who are preaching and teaching to have clean lives because the Holy Spirit cannot use unclean vessels. The Holy Spirit is also the one who will bring the verses that you are memorizing to your mind when you need them.

The Holy Spirit brings other provisions. You may have heard the term "spiritual gifts." A spiritual gift defines how the Holy Spirit works through your life. For example, Bible teachers are said to have the gift of teaching. Teaching is how the Holy Spirit works through those who lead the teaching ministry.

Christians may have several gifts. There are those who may have the gift of teaching, leadership, and intercession. The Bible says the Holy Spirit distributes these *"as He wills"* (1 Corinthians 12:11). He distributes these gifts so that we can be equipped to serve.

God has called you to be saved and to serve. He, like the most loving parent, grandparent, or guardian, has also provided the tools it takes for you to serve. We are not saved just to sit and soak up all we can learn. We receive spiritual food, then we exercise those spiritual gifts as we serve. The result is spiritual growth.

There are those who covet certain gifts because they believe they are more important. Every gift is just as important as the others. If you want to covet a gift, covet the gift of love. Every believer has this gift, and it is the *"more excellent way"* (1 Corinthians 12:31).

Many people believe that a talent is a spiritual gift. The problem is that unbelievers have talents, but they do not have gifts because they do not have "the Gift" (the Holy Spirit). One does not receive gifts until he/she receives the gift of the Holy Spirit. He/She does not receive Him until he/she decides to follow Jesus, seeks God's forgiveness, and invites Jesus to come in and take over his/her life. A talent can be transformed into a gift, but it is not automatically a gift.

I have a friend who has the gift of creative communication. He plays the guitar. For several years he used this talent to play music in nightclubs. After he asked Jesus into his life, however, he discontinued playing the nightclub music and began playing in church. There is no doubt in my mind that God's Spirit took a great talent and transformed it into a spiritual gift.

I have another friend who is a preacher. He did not grow up as a great communicator. He had an average personality and very little charisma. Today my friend is pastor of one of the fastest growing churches in the state where he lives. He is a testimony to how God can call and equip someone who does not have talents with the gifts needed to follow God's call.

God can turn talents into gifts, but He can also, through His Holy Spirit, provide gifts where no talent or ability exists. You may want to look at the talents you had prior to becoming a Christian, but also look beyond your talents and be available for whatever God wants to do in your life.

In Week Fourteen, you will learn more about spiritual gifts and the ways they are combined with both your personality and your life's focus to be used by God to help you to serve.

Your Daily Walk

Scripture: 1 Corinthians 12:1-11

As you read these verses today, you may not understand everything Paul is saying. I want these verses to introduce you to God's teachings about gifts.

Review:

- The Holy Spirit is "the G_____" God gives every believer.
- The g_____ define how the Holy Spirit wants to work through you.
- From the scripture reading for today, write down one spiritual gift: _____.

Journal: Write what God is doing in your life and how He is speaking to you.

_____

_____

_____

_____

_____

_____

_____

_____

_____

Prayer:

Pray that God will teach you how to both recognize and exercise your gifts.

_____

_____

_____

_____

_____

_____

Is there Protection?

Today is a good day for you to learn that salvation and service invite attacks. It is likely that you have already experienced attacks from the enemy, but you may not have identified what is happening to you. Christians need the protection that the Holy Spirit offers. The provisions come through the spiritual gifts, and the protection comes through the spiritual armor. Last week I introduced the spiritual armor. This week I want you to understand why you need the protection the armor gives. The rope that binds together God's provisions and protection is the Holy Spirit. He lives in us, works out of us and is there to protect us.

Many believers reach this point and become lukewarm in their spiritual walk for fear of what the devil might do. Fear not! Wouldn't we rather have Satan angry with us everyday than for God to be upset with us one day? Satan may have power, but God has much more than he does. Additionally, God offers protection from Satan. What are some keys to receiving God's protection?

First, Jesus said to pray that the Father would deliver you from "*the evil one*" (Matthew 6:13, NIV). There is no sense in seeking a battle that you can avoid. Know that the one place Satan does not want to be is close to God. The closer you are to God, the more distance you place between yourself and evil. Remember the discussion on the spiritual armor? The way to get close to God is to pray this seven-part prayer of the Spiritual armor:

1. "Father, help me to be a person of truth. 2. Guide my life to be a reflection of righteousness. 3. Help me to be prepared at all times to be willing to share the good news of Jesus. 4. Teach me to walk by faith, 5. to guard my mind, 6. and to memorize and be able to use your word. 7. Above all, Father, help me to listen to you so that I will know what to do. Do not allow me to quench the Holy Spirit who lives in me, convicts me and corrects me. I pray this prayer so that I will look like your Son, Jesus."

Second, pray for those friends and family members who are close to you. If you are close to God and experiencing His protection, then you may notice those who are close to you experiencing various kinds of trials. Pray for them as well. I might have trouble proving this theologically, but it seems that when I am close to God, Satan often attacks my church and those close to me. My guard is up, but I often get hit with "stray bullets" intended for those around me.

Third, understand that trials are not always bad. You have already learned that God works through the trials to help us to grow. However, understand that the goal of the evil one is not to bring us trials. He knows that trials can strengthen us. The last desire he has is for Christians to become strong. The goal of the evil one is to kill us. Remember those words of John 10:10, "*The thief (Satan) comes for the sole purpose of stealing our salvation, killing our witness and destroying our joy*" (LPP). He does not want to try us; he wants to go straight to the execution.

One day our lives will end. Numerous times I have listened as the Rev. Dr. Billy Graham quoted Hebrews 9:27, *"It is appointed unto men once to die, but after this the judgment"* (KJV). I would not think that many Christians would want it said at the judgment seat of Christ that they were saved, but they spent more of their lives fearing evil than fearing God. I would hope that we would want to hear these words from the Lord: *"Well done, good and faithful servant; you were faithful over a few things, I will make you ruler over many things. Enter into the joy of your Lord"* (Matthew 25:21, NKJ).

Your Daily Walk

Scripture: Ephesians 6:10-18

As you read the verses for today, understand that Paul did not tell us to put on the armor of God for no reason. We will need protection, and that protection is in our relationship to God

Memory verses: Remove the card that says "Ephesians 6:10-18" from your "To Learn" group and move it to your "Working to Memorize" group. Today you will be challenged to expand your memory. The memory verses are Ephesians 6:13-18. These six verses will change your spiritual life. Locate them, underline them, detach the card at the back of the book and begin to memorize them.

Review:

•What are three important prayers for protection?

1.   Pray that God will d_____ you from the evil one.

2.   Pray that God will d_____ your family and friends from evil.

3.   Pray that God will cause the t_____ to work for good, not bring you down.

Journal: Write what God is doing in your life and how He is speaking to you.

_____
_____
_____
_____
_____
_____
_____
_____
_____

Prayer:

Pray that God will teach you how serve Him without fear.

_____
_____
_____
_____
_____

Can I Promote?

Believers can look inside their lives and know the Holy Spirit is there to provide for them to serve, using the spiritual gifts that He gives to them. He protects them as they serve through the spiritual armor. He also promotes the kingdom of God through their service as they use the spiritual fruit.

Galatians 5:22-23 introduces us to the first nine parts to the spiritual fruit. These are love, joy, peace, patience, kindness, goodness, faithfulness, gentleness, and self-control. When God's Holy Spirit is working in our lives, then we are the greatest billboard that exists on this earth. Christians can be the best or worst advertisements that God has. He wants us to be the best. He wants us to be promoters of the kingdom. Jesus told us to let our light shine so that people would see the good that we do and that we would use the opportunity to point people to Him (Matthew 5:16).

As a believer, you may think that God wants you to work on each part individually. I have some important news. The spiritual fruit is not the goal of the Christian's life, but a gauge of the kind of relationship that he/she has with God through the Holy Spirit. Displaying the fruit of the spirit should not be a chore to accomplish but a supernatural overflow of a life that is grounded in God's word and built on the proper foundation.

First, and very important, the word "fruit" from the Greek New Testament is singular. These nine parts are part of the whole fruit. One cannot separate them, and our work is to love others, express joy, live in peace, walk patiently, practice kindness, work goodness, demonstrate faithfulness, exhibit gentleness, and be self-controlled. Conversely, one cannot be faithful to the eight other parts, but lack patience. We must see the spiritual fruit as a whole, and gauge our relationship to the Father based on whether we are positive promoters of the entire fruit.

Second, this is called the fruit of the Spirit, not the fruit of the believer. He, the Holy Spirit, is the one who flows out of us in the nine areas of the fruit. Trying to demonstrate the fruit of the Spirit from a shallow relationship that is on a plateau or declining is one of the most unpleasant struggles that a Christian could face. Let me give a word of caution. If you are in a church where there are few facades, and many people are genuinely changing and growing in their spiritual walk but you are not, then one of three things will happen. You will either remove the mask and get back to growing, leave and go find a place where it is easier to fake the fruit, or stay away from worshiping with believers altogether. Do not leave! Stay, take off the mask and work to build a relationship with God that is mature, vibrant and real. In a church where few masks are worn, the Christians will not chastise you for being where you are; they will encourage you to get to where God is blessing. The chastisement will come from those in churches who are accustomed to wearing masks or from the world that will mark you a hypocrite. Stay with believers who know they are imperfect just like you.

Some years ago I discontinued wearing a coat and tie on Sunday. I did not instruct others to do so, but many others followed. Initially, I recognized that there were those that we needed to reach who could not afford many nice clothes. However, there was an unexpected result. The masks came off. Our church learned that God is not as interested in how we look on the outside but what is happening on the inside. Most of us stopped looking at others and started looking inside our lives.

Do not try to fake a spiritual walk. Continue to build your relationship, spend time with God, listen to Him through the Bible and watch how He, the Holy Spirit, will love through you as never before, give you a joy unspeakable, provide a peace that passes understanding, give you a kind and tender heart, lead you to do good works, help you to remain faithful, provide you with a gentle spirit, teach you how to live under control, and show you how to lead people to Jesus.

Your Daily Walk

Scripture: Galatians 5:22-23; Proverbs 11:30; John 15:8

Underline each of these in your Bible.

Review:

•What parts are in the fruit of the Spirit:

1. L_____; 2. J_____; 3. P_____; 4. P_____;
5. K_____; 6. G_____; 7. F_____;
8. G_____; 9. Self-c_____; and 10. S_____.

Journal: Write what God is doing in your life and how He is speaking to you.

_____
_____
_____
_____
_____
_____
_____
_____
_____
_____
_____
_____
_____
_____

Prayer:

Pray that God will teach you how to be a positive promoter for Him. Pray for a growing relationship so that the fruit of the Spirit will be seen in your life.

_____
_____
_____
_____
_____
_____

Can I Share?

Week 7, Day 5 - Thursday - Date: ____/____/_____

Yesterday we discussed Paul's nine parts to the spiritual fruit. If you add the fruit of souls that Jesus talked about in John 15:8, then you have an even ten. I suggest that the fruit of souls could be a tenth part of the fruit of the Spirit. When you and I are in touch with God's Holy Spirit, then the overflow of people coming to Christ through us is inevitable. In John 15:16 Jesus calls this the *"fruit that remains."*

Many people believe that telling others about Jesus requires extensive training and great spiritual maturity. Jesus called Andrew to follow Him, and Andrew went to his brother, Simon, and brought Him to Jesus. Andrew had not been discipled; he had not joined a Bible study class, and had yet to hear a sermon. He simply met Jesus and shared Jesus.

The woman at the well met Jesus. She left the well, went to the city and started witnessing. She, like Andrew, had not been trained. Being a positive witness for Jesus is not a matter of being able, but being available for God to use you. Resist the trap of allowing the fear of witnessing to produce excuses in your life. Let me help you with your fear. I believe, and others have affirmed, that God has given me a special ability and desire to lead others to Jesus and disciple people to lead others to Jesus. Yet, every time I talk to an unbeliever, I have a healthy level of fear that causes me to rely on God and allow His Holy Spirit to witness through me.

More Abundant LIFE teaches you that witnessing is an integral part of your Christian walk. Witnessing comes from Jesus' Great Commission: *"Therefore go and make disciples of all nations, baptizing them in the name of the Father and of the Son and of the Holy Spirit, and teaching them to obey everything I have commanded you..."* (Matthew 28:19–20, NIV). Literally, verse 19 begins, "As you go..." or "*As you continue on your journey,* (from the Greek word *poreuomai* [pronounced po-roo-o-mi]), *make disciples....*" The only imperative in these two verses is to *"make disciples."* These verses were not directed at preachers and evangelists. These verses comprise Jesus' "Great Commission" to every Christian of every generation.

Believers need to learn that Jesus assumed that we would go. As we are going, His command is to make disciples. Making disciples begins with believers sharing their faith. The short answer is that you can share. You can tell people what has happened and is happening in your life. You can tell them about this study that you are working through. You can invite them to your Bible study class. You can invite them to worship with you or to attend a special event at your church. You can share!

You can share because you are a disciple, and you are growing as a disciple. Discipleship is a personal, lifelong, obedient relationship with Jesus Christ in which He transforms your character into Christ likeness, changes your values into Kingdom values and involves you in His mission in the home, the church, and the world. These are some of the goals of *More Abundant LIFE*. As you learn how to grow as a disciple and share what Christ is doing in your life, you are living out the commission that Jesus gives every Christian. Tomorrow you will learn what to say when someone wants to know how to become a Christian. It was difficult for me to share with the first person I witnessed to who prayed to receive Christ into his life. I did not know what to say, and I stumbled through a few verses of scripture. I determined as a pastor that those whom I serve will have every opportunity to learn how to share the gospel so that the Holy Spirit can do His work and lead them into the Kingdom. Tomorrow may be your first step in a process to become an effective witness for Jesus.

Your Daily Walk

Scripture: Luke 14:23

Jesus told us to go everywhere and compel people to come.

Memory verse: Remove the card that says "Luke 14:23" from your "To Learn" group and move it to your "Working to Memorize" group. Luke 14:23 is the fourteenth verse or passage overall and your final verse for the first half of *More Abundant LIFE*.

Turn to this verse in your Bible and underline it.

Review:

•Who are two New Testament witnesses who shared their witness but were not trained yet? A_____ and the w_____ at the w_____.

•Can you share your witness? Y_____.

•Will you? _____

Journal: Write what God is doing in your life and how He is speaking to you.

_____
_____
_____
_____
_____
_____
_____
_____
_____
_____

Prayer:

Pray that God will give you the courage to be a verbal witness for Him.

_____
_____
_____
_____
_____
_____
_____

What do I Say?

The first week of *More Abundant LIFE* encourages believers to present their first public witness through baptism. Your witness begins there, but it does not stop at the waters of baptism. The witness of a growing Christian will grow with him/her. Your witness should be given often. It should be both a life-style and verbal witness.

Believers often question which is more important, our living witness or our verbal witness? My response is to ask them which is more important when they are 36,000 feet off the ground flying to another city, the right wing of the airplane or the left wing? The plane needs both wings to stay in the air. The Christian needs both his/her living and verbal witness to be complete.

The next question new believers ask is, "What do I say?" Week 12 of *More Abundant LIFE* will provide a more complete guideline to being a verbal witness, but for now let me return to the LIFE presentation from the first week.

To be a witness, one must have seen and heard. Without personal knowledge, it is hearsay. A witness has personally experienced Jesus. When Peter and John were confronted by the rulers, elders, scribes and priests in Acts 4, they responded by telling them *"For we cannot help speaking about what we have seen and heard."* These leaders supposed that the disciples had made up a story. When the leaders questioned them, they realized that the disciples were eye witnesses.

Sharing Your Experience

When telling someone about the experience that you have had with Christ, you may want to say something like this:

"There was a time in my life when I was not certain I would go to heaven. Then I learned that 1. God Loved me. The Bible taught me that God is love (1 John 4:8), not that I loved Him, but that He loved me (1 John 4:10) and sent Jesus to die for me and save me (John 3:16).

The problem is that 2. People are Imperfect. I learned that I had sinned and fallen short of God's standard of perfection (Romans 3:23). If I had stayed that way, the penalty would have been spiritual death with no opportunity to go to Heaven (Romans 6:23).

The solution is that 3. Jesus offers Forgiveness (Ephesians 1:7). I learned that I needed to change my life's direction and follow Him in order to receive His forgiveness. I did that one day. I prayed, asked for God's forgiveness, acknowledged that I could not get to heaven without His Son, and invited Jesus to come into my life (Romans 10:9) and be the Lord of my life.

Now 4. I have Eternal life. I know that if today were the last day of my life, I would spend eternity with God in heaven (1 John 5:13).[10]

There are times when I share with unbelievers these four points of *It's LIFE* and the related scriptures, and God's Spirit causes the person to whom I am talking to want to become a Christian. When this happens, I lead them to lift up this prayer to God:

"Heavenly Father, I believe that you love me and gave your Son to die for me. I also know I have sinned and need to be forgiven. Lord Jesus, I want to turn from sin and my past, and ask you to forgive me. Please come into my life, be the Lord of my life, and give me eternal life. Thank-you for forgiving me, coming into my life, and giving me eternal life. Amen."

The above prayer can be a guide for you. If you are available for God to use you, someone will likely ask you to tell him how to become a Christian. You can lead him/her to pray and be confident that God will be looking at his/her intent. If he/she wants to turn and trust in Jesus, then He will come into his/her life and give him/her eternal life.

Your Daily Walk

Scripture: 1 John 5:13

Turn to the verse for today. Underline it and remember that we can know that we have eternal life.

Review:

• The most important words you will share when witnessing are words from the Bible.

• Learning an organized plan will help you to remember what you need to say, give you more confidence to share and provide something you can teach others.

• You and I can share, but God is the one who saves.

Journal: Write what God is doing in your life and how He is speaking to you. Do you have a desire to share your Christian witness? _____

_____

_____

_____

_____

_____

_____

_____

_____

Prayer:

Pray that God will help you remember how to share your faith.

_____

_____

_____

_____

_____

_____

_____

_____

A Time to Recommit

Week 7, Day 7 - Saturday - Date: ____/____/_____

Today is the conclusion of the seventh week and the first part of *More Abundant LIFE*. Notice that today is day seven of week seven. The number seven in the Bible is used to represent "perfection." At this point you are not complete, but you are on track to be more like Jesus, and He was perfect.

Take time to catch up, and reflect on what you have learned in these first weeks. If you missed any days, then return, read and recover the information that you overlooked. Be certain that you move to the second section of *More Abundant LIFE*. I would like to how God is working in your life. If you are led, please take a moment to email me at **lawrence.phipps@itslifeministry.com**. I want to read the testimony of what God is doing in your life.

Keep going. The next seven weeks will take you deeper into your study of the seven pillars of faith.

Highlights from Week 7:

Read through each day of Week 7 and record a teaching from each day:

- Monday   - _____

_____

- Tuesday   - _____

_____

- Wednesday-_____

_____

- Thursday   - _____

_____

- Friday   - _____

_____

Journal:

Take time to write in your journal. Write down ideas and record events that are impacting your life in Christ. Record the victories and the struggles, the concepts you are learning and those you still do not understand.

_____

_____

_____

_____

_____

Prayer: As you talk to God, remember to **a**cknowledge, **a**dore, **a**ccept, **a**sk, **a**dmit any sin, **a**lign with God, **a**void the enemy, **a**ccompany God, and **a**ppreciate His blessings.

Reminder: Tomorrow is the traditional day to worship God. Whether your worship time is Friday night, Saturday or Sunday, ask God to help you to prepare before worship. Do not wait until your day of worship to rest and get ready. Prepare in advance so that you will get the most from worship.

Week 8

Build your Connection!

The Lord said to Moses, *"Speak to that rock before their eyes and it will pour out its water. So Moses raised his arm and struck the rock."* Moses wasn't listening! Previously God told him to strike the rock in order to get water. This time He told him to speak to it. Moses had predetermined what he believed was God's will, and it cost him the ability to go into the Promised Land. *"The Lord said to Moses, 'Because you did not trust in me enough to honor me as holy in the sight of the Israelites, you will not bring this community into the land I give them'"* (from Numbers 20).

The first pillar of the Christian's walk is **Prayer.** You have learned that prayer is a conversation between two who love each other. Prayer includes speaking and listening. Week 8 is the first week of the second part of *More Abundant LIFE.* This week will help serious disciples learn to strengthen their personal prayer life. Your **Priority Time** with God is an important time to speak and listen to Him. Have you discovered an optimum priority time? If you have not, take a moment and ask God to help you understand the blessing a child of God gets when he/she sets aside a time to be with a loving, heavenly Father. You are deciding whether or not you will enter God's promised land for you.

Be Committed to Worship

Week 8, Day 1 - Sunday - Date: _____/_____/_____

Today launches the final fifty-one days of your first one hundred as a growing believer in Jesus Christ. As you grow, know that worship is not something you watch others do; it is something that you as a believer do. You may believe that your voice is not advanced enough to sing. Learn that God is looking at the heart, not listening to the tune. You may be concerned that others are listening. Remember that you are not in worship for them, but for Him. On the other hand, you may know or discover that you have a great voice. My friend David Wingate, a graduate of Julliard, was professor of voice at Florida State University and sang in the Florida State Opera. He was saved, and then God turned his talent into a gift that he has used mightily for His glory. God may be turning old talents into new gifts. You may have been in worship, but now you need to think about joining a choir, praise team, or praise band, or playing an instrument in worship or for other groups (preschool through adults) in the church.

Your worship notes have changed. Worship includes giving and receiving. Pay attention to what you do in worship today. The Bible says, *"Therefore by Him let us continually **offer the sacrifice of praise** to God, that is, the fruit of our lips, giving thanks to His name."* (Hebrews 13:15, NKJ) Ask yourself these questions:

1. Did I give anything to God in worship today? ____Yes ____No
2. Did I offer an acceptable sacrifice of praise? ____Yes ____No
3. What did I receive from God? _____

The title of the pastor's message:_____
The main Bible text:_____
The main points of the pastor's message: _____

_____
_____
_____
_____
_____
_____
_____
_____

This is what I learned that I can apply to my life:_____

_____
_____

Prayer: Ask God to help you apply what you have learned today.

_____
_____

How to Strengthen Your Priority Time - Part 1
Week 8, Day 2 - Monday - Date: ____/____/_____

The purpose of Week 8 is to help believers strengthen their lives of prayer. This week is entitled "Build Your Connection." This connection is conversing with God. Much of the insight God has given me about prayer came while writing *Praying in Faith* and *A Forty Day Experience*. When **LifeWay Christian Resources** asked me to write *Praying in Faith*, I thought it was because of what I knew about prayer. As I wrote the book, I began to realize that God wanted me to write the book because of what He was going to teach *me* about prayer.

Several years ago, God revealed to me an important advantage to having a daily priority time with Him. I realized that virtually every new biblical insight I had received had come to me during my devotional priority time. Most new insights did not come while I was reading my Bible study lesson, or preparing to teach or getting ready to preach. When I make an appointment to talk to God and hear from God, He provides incredible understanding.

Have a FRUITFUL Priority Time

Week 1 of *More Abundant LIFE* teaches believers that it is important to have and to keep their daily appointment with God. Paul said in Colossians 1:10 *"That you may walk worthy of the Lord, fully pleasing Him, being **fruitful** in every good work and increasing in the knowledge of God"* (NKJ). We, as believers, become fruitful when our knowledge of God increases. We increase our knowledge of Him when we spend time with Him.

I have developed an acrostic that will be used during the next three days to help you remember what it takes to have a priority time that bears fruit. There are five letters in fruit and five principles to help improve your time with God. Each principle begins with one of the letters of FRUIT. I will discuss the first two principles today, the second one tomorrow, and the final two on day Wednesday.

Principle 1 - Be Faithful

The Bible says that God is faithful. *"God, who has called you into fellowship with his Son Jesus Christ our Lord, is faithful"* (1 Corinthians 1:9, NIV). If we are to be like Him, then we need to be faithful. Faithfulness to God impacts our entire lives. Christians who learn to be faithful to God also become faithful husbands, wives, students, church members, employers, employees, neighbors and citizens. One evidence of God's Spirit living in us is faithfulness. *"But the fruit of the Spirit is love, joy, peace, patience, kindness, goodness, <u>faithfulness</u>..."* (Galatians 5:22, NIV). Be faithful to spend time with God, and He will faithfully work through you and bless you.

Principle 2 - Read

Your priority time should be balanced between speaking and listening. During the first few weeks of *More Abundant LIFE,* you learned that the Christian's greatest listening tool is the Bible. Take God's word into your priority time. Devotion guides can help you to understand the Bible but should never be a substitute for reading the Bible. An important part of *More Abundant LIFE* is scripture. My goal is not to tell you what God's word says, but to show you. Many believers make the mistake of trying to live off the milk of the word (what others tell them about the Bible). Let me encourage you to mix the milk with solid food (what you get on your own). Open up your Bible!

Fruit-bearing believers faithfully spend time with God and read His word. The next step will be to understand what you are reading.

Your Daily Walk

Your Daily Walk has changed. Each day there will be one scripture passage listed for you to read. There will continue to be two memory verses each week., and they will be designated as in previous weeks. Additionally, there will be an opportunity to check your **Application** or make application from what you are studying.

The **Journal** and **Prayer** portions will be your opportunity to keep a daily journal of what God is doing and what you are requesting from God without the instructions or prompting that we provided in the first seven weeks. There will be more room to journal. I hope that you will begin increasing the record of both what you are learning and what our Father, Jesus and Holy Spirit are doing in and through your life.

Scripture:
2 Timothy 3:16-17

Application:
When was your priority time today? _____

Journal: _____

_____

_____

_____

_____

_____

_____

_____

_____

_____

_____

_____

_____

Prayer: _____

_____

_____

_____

_____

How to Strengthen Your Priority Time - Part 2

Be Faithful

Read

Principle 3 - Understand and Use Scripture

One of the most rewarding aspects of prayer is to find a promise in the Bible and incorporate it into your prayer. Several years ago, I was leading a team of five people to Uzbekistan to disciple the Christians in that country to share their faith using Evangelism Explosion. We left the United States with a visa that would get us to Moscow but not Uzbekistan. I sat in a chair in a makeshift Uzbek embassy (located on an alley street). I had just been denied five visas, I began to pray: "Lord, You promised that if we seek first your kingdom and righteousness, then you would add everything to us. Father, we are here by faith to do your will. We ask that You provide the visas." Within minutes a man walked into the room, asked the other man (in Russian) why I was there. He then overruled the man who was not going to supply the visas. Within hours we were on the plane to Uzbekistan. The verse that gave me confidence as I prayed was Matthew 6:33. *"But seek ye first the kingdom of God, and his righteousness; and all these things shall be added unto you."* (KJV) I did not have my Bible with me, but I had memorized Matthew 6:33, and God's Spirit helped me to recall the verse.

You have been guided in *More Abundant LIFE* to memorize the word of God. One reason we memorize and learn scripture is to be able to recall it and use it when we pray. The purpose of using scripture in prayer is not to remind God of what He says in the Bible but to remind us. Knowing and searching for verses that relate to our needs help us to know the character of God and pray according to the will of God.

The *Spiritual Armor*, in Ephesians 6, lists the *"Sword of the Spirit"* (the word of God) immediately before "Prayer." It is as if God is saying: "Take up the *'Sword of the Spirit'*, which is the word of God, and pray what you are reading in this word to Me." Here are some other verses you can learn and pray.

1. When you are following God, but the task seems impossible, pray Philippians 4:13: *"I can do everything through Christ who gives me strength"*.

2. When there is a national tragedy, then pray 2 Chronicles 7:14: *"If My people who are called by My name will humble themselves, and pray and seek My face, and turn from their wicked ways, then I will hear from heaven, and will forgive their sin and heal their land"* (NKJ).

3. When trials or personal tragedy come upon you, then follow 1 Thessalonians 5:18: *"In every thing give thanks: for this is the will of God in Christ Jesus concerning you."* (KJV); and pray Romans 8:28: *"And we know that all things work together for good to those who love God, to those who are the called according to His purpose."* (NKJ).

4. When you cannot rest, then pray and claim Jeremiah 6:16b: *"...ask for the ancient paths, ask where the good way is, and walk in it, and you will find*

rest for your souls..." (NIV)

5.   When you believe you are in danger, then pray Psalm 12:7: *"You shall keep them, O LORD, You shall preserve them from this generation forever"* (NKJ).

6.   When you are trying to discover the truth about a situation, then pray Mark 4:22:   *"For whatever is hidden is meant to be disclosed, and whatever is concealed is meant to be brought out into the open"* (NIV).

7.   When you know of someone who is struggling with whether he/she is going to return to righteousness, pray Matthew 21:44, *"And whoever falls on this stone will be broken; but on whomever it falls, it will grind him to powder"* (NKJ). We want people to be broken before they are crushed by their sin.

The more you read the Bible and understand God's promises, the more you will learn to use scripture as you pray. Knowing that God has already spoken concerning a need you or someone else has will strengthen your belief that God will answer as you pray.

Your Daily Walk

Scripture:
2 Chronicles 7:14

Memory verse: Remove the card that says "2 Chronicles 7:14" from your "To Learn" group and move it to your "Working to Memorize" group. 2 Chronicles 7:14 is your first memory verse for Week 8.

Application:
What need do you have today? _____
Do you know a verse to meet that need? If yes, then write it here. If no, then ask a pastor or teacher for help.

Journal: _____

_____
_____
_____
_____
_____
_____
_____
_____
_____
_____
_____

Prayer: As you pray today, find one verse of promise and pray it to the Lord:

_____
_____
_____
_____
_____

How to Strengthen Your Priority Time - Part 3

Week 8, Day 4 - Wednesday - Date: ____/____/_____

Be **F**aithful
Read
Use Scripture
Principle 4 - Invite God

Your prayer life and priority time can be fruitful only if you invite God to guide your time. Your priority time is not just a time to learn about God and talk to God. Your priority time must be time spent with God. You learned in the first part of *More Abundant LIFE* that God's Spirit lives in Christians. Unfortunately, many of us act as if He is thousands of miles away.

You may want to begin your priority time by praying, "God, I do not want these minutes to be wasted. I do not want to act as if you are far away. I want to feel you near. I know you live in me. I want to talk and listen to you. Please help me to make you the focus of this time and not me."

We have learned that when we invite God into our priority time, we recognize His presence for the rest of the day. If our priority times are early in the day, then we experience and recognize His presence through the entire day. Those who have a priority time in the morning discover that when a problem arises God is already working to solve the problem. When there is no early priority time and a problem develops, we have to stop and invite God to help. Every time the latter happens, it consumes a greater amount of time than if we had the early priority time.

It is also important to note that the consistency of your priority time is more important than its length. It is better to spend a few minutes early in each day than longer periods every other day.

Be **F**aithful
Read
Use Scripture
Invite God
Principle 5 - **T**ake Notes

How was the Bible written? Someone took notes. They recorded what God did and said, and it became a record of God's magnificent work and power.

Faithfully keep a journal of insights, prayers and answered prayer. There will be times when you wonder if God is listening. Return to your notes, and you will be reminded of how He faithfully answered prayers in the past. Jesus felt abandoned on the cross. He said, *"My God, my God, why have you forsaken me?"* (Matthew 27:46, KJV). He was quoting Psalm 22. The rest of the Psalm says, *"Yet you are enthroned as the Holy One; you are the praise of Israel. In you our fathers put their trust; they trusted and you delivered them. They cried to you and were saved; in you they trusted and were not disappointed."* (Psalm 22:3-5). He felt forsaken, but He returned to His mental notes and knew

113

that God had been with Him in the past and would deliver Him. Jesus placed His faith in the Father who had been there in the past and His Father delivered Him. What a deliverance the resurrection was!

Your notes record what God is doing in your life. They will one day help you to recall how God worked, and when you read them, give you the faith that He will continue to work in the future. Through this study you have been provided a journal. After this study you may want to buy one from a bookstore or keep one in your computer. If you keep a computer journal, be certain to regularly save it to disk or tape. Have a fruitful priority time by being faithful, reading the word, using scripture, inviting God and taking notes. He is at work.

Your Daily Walk

Scripture:
  Psalm 5:3
Application:
  Spend time with God, and you can expect Him to answer when you pray.
Journal: _____

_____
_____
_____
_____
_____
_____
_____
_____
_____
_____
_____
_____
_____
_____
_____

Prayer: _____

_____
_____
_____
_____
_____
_____
_____
_____
_____

How Can I Improve My Connection?
Week 8, Day 5 - Thursday - Date: ____/____/_____

How far do you want to grow as a Christian? How powerful do you want your life of prayer to become? Matthew 17 tells the story of Jesus' working the miracle of mental and spiritual healing in a man's life. The disciples wanted to know why they were not able to do what He did. Jesus replied that to do what He had done requires "prayer and fasting" (Matthew 17:21, NIV).

You have learned what it means to pray, but what is fasting? Many believe that to fast is not to eat. Fasting is much broader and more meaningful than simply missing a meal or series of meals. The literal meaning of fasting is to "move fast toward God." The thought was that the Christian is so interested in *moving* toward God that he/she neglects to eat a meal, eat a dessert, see a movie or attend a pleasurable event or activity. Today's study will provide background for two kinds of fasts and instructions to lead the reader to observe his/her first fast.

Intentional Fast

A fast is an intentional fast when it is a planned event. Matthew 6:16 records Jesus saying, *"When you fast, do not look somber as the hypocrites do, for they disfigure their faces to show men they are fasting. I tell you the truth, they have received their reward in full."* (NIV) Notice that He says *when* you fast, not *if* you fast. It is obvious that Jesus believed that fasting would be a part of the lives of His disciples. The next two verses, Matthew 6:17-18 instruct the believer about what he/she should not do and should do as he/she fasts. *"But you, when you fast, anoint your head and wash your face, so that you do not appear to men to be fasting, but to your Father who is in the secret place; and your Father who sees in secret will reward you openly."* (NKJ)

The most powerful fasts are not designed because you need or want something. The greatest fast is one you plan in order to spend time with God. You may choose to fast from food in order to spend breakfast, lunch and/or dinner time reading the Bible and praying. When I fast for the purpose of getting to know God, I discover that when I have a personal need or I need to intercede for others, then answers come more quickly. However, my fasts are not for the purpose of boasting about my spirituality or getting recognition. Jesus taught that if we fast to bring attention to ourselves, then our fast is hypocritical.

Unintentional Fast

When a believer is busy doing God's work and neglects a personal pleasure, then he/she has fasted. It may not be planned, but it is still powerful. There have been times in my Christian life when I was busy doing God's work or getting close to Him. I have missed meals, athletic events and other activities that would have given me great pleasure. Every instance of fasting, whether intentional or unintentional, has been met with blessings.

Today's daily walk may introduce you to your first Christian fast. You may have already experienced an unintentional fast, but let me encourage you to plan a fast. Here are some guidelines.

1. Plan the time (try to choose a time in the next two days).

2. Select the type of fast. Decide to miss a meal, a night of television or other activity you enjoy.

3. Spend your fasting time with God. Open your Bible to John 17. Did you know that Jesus prayed for you in John 17? Listen to Jesus as you read this word, and then talk to God. There may be other passages that are meaningful to you that you want to read in this special time of building your relationship.

4. Ask God to meet a specific need of yours, your family or a friend.

5. Record your prayer below and record when and how God answers.

Your Daily Walk

Scripture:

John 17 - Read the entire prayer. It is the prayer of Jesus to the Father about His followers. This is His prayer for you and me.

Application:

I am scheduling the following day and time to fast: ___/___/_____;
from ____:_____ to ____:____.

Journal: _____

_____
_____
_____
_____
_____
_____
_____
_____
_____
_____
_____
_____
_____
_____
_____
_____
_____

Prayer: _____

_____
_____
_____
_____
_____
_____
_____

What Does it mean to "Agree" in Prayer?

Christians are called to have a personal priority time with God. Jesus, as recorded in Matthew 6:6 says, *"But you, when you pray, go into your room, and when you have shut your door, pray to your Father who is in the secret place; and your Father who sees in secret will reward you openly"* (NKJ). It is necessary to have a time to be alone with God. However, Christians are also called to pray with others. In Matthew 18:19-20, Jesus said, *"Again I say to you that if two of you **agree** on earth concerning anything that they ask, it will be done for them by My Father in heaven. For where two or three are gathered together in My name, I am there in the midst of them"* (NKJ). I often wondered why agreement was important. The Bible tells us to agree, but it does not specifically explain why agreement is important. After much prayer and years of study, I have discovered that there are four possible reasons why praying with others can strengthen our prayers:

1.   When many people are praying, the chances are increased that someone is lined up with God. Sometimes Christians talk to God but have sin in their lives. The early studies in *More Abundant LIFE* described how sin blocks communication. God is not obligated to listen to one who is guilty of unconfessed sin. Neither can the one who has unconfessed and unforgiven sin in his/her life hear God. The goal is to confess our sin and receive forgiveness; then we can ask and God will hear, and we can hear from God. Inviting others to pray with us may help us or them to line up with God so that our prayers can be answered.

2.   Agreement in prayer assures God the Father that His children are gathering. Parents who have provided a loving family environment are pleased when their children come together. Some families rent vacation houses each year to gather and fellowship together. The children may be married and have children of their own. There is a glow on the parents' faces as they see the love and admiration the siblings have for one another. God has provided the perfect family environment. When His children come together with love in an atmosphere of agreement, the Father shows up. They agree to ask for something that will help others and honor Him, and He gives it to them. God loves for His children to get together.

3.   When we pray together, we are being obedient to the commands of Christ. You will recall that Jesus, in Matthew 28:20, instructed believers to teach other believers to obey what He had commanded them. God honors those who obey His Son. Jesus told us to agree and gather to pray, and we should obey.

There are times in my Christian life when I enlisted a prayer partner or partners. I discovered that when I did not know how to pray or did not know I needed to pray for something, they did. God honors agreement.

Week twelve will introduce you to a powerful verse about agreement. There is a special strength that God gives when people come together to pray.

4.   A final important idea of agreement is when the church gathers to pray. God works mightily when the local congregation of believers is willing to come together and call out to God on behalf of an individual, family, missionary, or the nation. In 2003 when people were being shot and killed by the D.C. sniper, our church, in both Sunday worship hours, came to the altar to pray for the "hidden things to be revealed" and that the authorities would find the sniper. That night a Christian trucker pulled into a truck stop, spotted the car, arrested the two men, and the killing ended. Every church that responded to God's call to pray that day had the opportunity to rejoice as we did that we had been obedient and God answered. When your church is called to prayer, be certain that you show up.

Your Daily Walk

Scripture:
>   Matthew 18:19-20

Memory verses: Remove the card that says "Matthew 18:19-20" from your "To Learn" group and move it to your "Working to Memorize" group. Matthew 18:19-20 is your second memory passage for this week.

Application:
>   Who can you meet and pray within the next week?_____
When will you pray with a partner? _____

Journal: _____

_____

_____

_____

_____

_____

_____

_____

_____

_____

_____

_____

_____

_____

_____

_____

Prayer: _____

_____

_____

_____

_____

_____

_____

_____

A Time to Reflect, Recover and Review
Week 8, Day 7 - Saturday - Date: _____/_____/_____

There is a time each week when disciples need to slow down, catch up and reflect on what they have learned. If you have done each day's assignment as designed, then enjoy this time of rest and review. If you missed a day or two, then return, read and recover the information that you overlooked. Each day is important. Every study is designed to build on the foundation, Jesus, and construct the seven pillars of a Christian's faith: Prayer, Worship, Witness, Bible Study, Discipleship, Fellowship and Service.

Highlights from Week 8:
Read through each day of Week 8 and record a teaching from each day:
- Monday   - _____

- Tuesday   - _____

- Wednesday- _____

- Thursday   - _____

- Friday   - _____

Journal:
Take time to write in your journal. Write down ideas and record events that are impacting your life in Christ. Record the victories and the struggles, the concepts you are learning and those you still do not understand.

_____

_____

_____

_____

_____

_____

Prayer: Talk to God today. Listen to what He is saying to you.

Remember: Tomorrow is the traditional day to worship God. Whether your worship time is Friday night, Saturday or Sunday, ask God to help you to prepare before worship. Do not wait until your day of worship to rest and get ready. Prepare in advance so that you will get the most from worship.

Week 9

Build your Covenant

A paraphrase of a real life story

"Let's change the subject," the woman in the fourth chapter of the Gospel of John implied. "I can tell you are a good man. I come from a good family. Let me tell you about how my family worshiped in this church. Let me share with you a part of my past and you will get a glimpse of what I am comfortable with."

"Let's not change the subject," Jesus indicated. "Your family's worship is partly to blame for your having five husbands and to now be living with a man who is not your husband. Worship for you has been a ritual. I want it to become connected to a relationship that you can have with the heavenly Father. I want you to join in Spirit-filled worship that is real and brings about life-change" (from John 4 - a paraphrased version of the conversation between Jesus and the woman at the well).

The second pillar of a Christian's life is **Worship**. Week 9 is designed to help you to grow in your admiration and reverence of God. Have you begun to learn how to worship? Do you understand that you are worshiping God? Ask God to use this week to help you learn to honor Him. Begin to build a covenant relationship that will pass on spirit-filled worship to those who come after you.

Be Committed to Worship

Sunday is a day of corporate worship. Most churches also offer small group Bible studies. Find time to honor God. Find a place where Christians are encouraged to worship, and the lost are invited to come to Christ.

Take your copy of *More Abundant LIFE* and take notes. The more you write, the more you will retain.

Worship includes giving and receiving. Pay attention to what you do in worship today. The Bible says, *"Therefore by Him let us continually **offer the sacrifice of praise** to God, that is, the fruit of our lips, giving thanks to His name."* (Hebrews 13:15, NKJ) Ask yourself these questions:

1. Did I give anything to God in worship today? ___Yes ___No
2. Did I offer an acceptable sacrifice of praise? ___Yes ___No
3. What did I receive from God? _____

The title of the pastor's message:_____
The main Bible text:_____
The main points of the pastor's message: _____

_____
_____
_____
_____
_____
_____
_____
_____
_____
_____

This is what I learned that I can apply to my life: _____

_____
_____
_____

Prayer: "Lord, help me to apply your word to my life."

_____
_____
_____
_____

Will My Worship Change?

Nearly two hundred people were in the room when I asked if anyone wanted to share a word of testimony. Tim stood and gave God thanks for saving him fifteen years ago. He explained that in fifteen years he had read and continued to memorize parts of the Bible. He had learned how to witness and was leading people to Christ. He had been discipled and was discipling others. He told us that he had grown in his prayer life and had learned to love and serve. "However," he said, "I recently discovered that while every area of my Christian walk had changed, I was still worshiping the same way I worshiped when I was saved." The great news from Tim is that he is now growing in worship, too.

There is no evidence in the Bible to indicate that any of the seven pillars of growth needs to remain the same. If we are to grow spiritually, we must grow in prayer, witness, Bible study, discipleship, fellowship, service and yes, worship. One of the first realities *More Abundant LIFE* discussed was the tragedy that a Christian's growth is stunted when he/she has a narrow base. Remember, the wider the base the higher the growth. Skyscrapers must have a strong foundation and a broad base. Growing in worship will help you to broaden your base and become a Christian skyscraper.

Not long ago I was in worship with a friend from years gone by. We had worshiped together many times during the 1980's. As we sang, the words of the songs were projected on overhead screens. I noticed my friend was still holding, staring at and singing from a hymnal. He knew the words, but he stared at the book. During worship he was asked to lead in prayer. As he began to pray, I realized that with almost two decades of distance between us I could almost pray his prayer for him. I was stunned and saddened that my friend's worship had remained the same.

My experience gave me an opportunity to thank God for putting people in my life who have helped me to grow in worship. When I was interviewed about being the pastor of a new church in Alabama, I was asked about my attitude concerning worship. My reply was that I did not want to sing the old songs every week but neither did I want the drums. By 2013 the songs were a mixture of the old and new, but the church has five drum sets in five different auditoriums. I have grown to understand that people should not come to worship to hear the pastor, but the pastor and congregation should worship in order to honor, humbly bow, and prayerfully listen to God. My worship is changing.

Paul, in Romans 12:1 says, *"...offer your bodies as living sacrifices...This is your spiritual act of <u>service</u>."* (NIV) The next verse says, *"Do not conform to the traditions of this world, but <u>change</u> and keep on changing. As you change, then you will grow toward God's perfect will, and that pleases Him"* (LPP).

Be prepared to grow in worship. Be prepared to serve God in worship. Be open to change as God directs you to change. When we are a "perfect" worshipers, then we can cease changing our worship.

A 1980's prayer partner of mine was a demonstrative worshiper. Unfortunately, as he would lift his hands, people would stare at him. As we gathered to pray one week, he said, "I look forward to the day that I can feel comfortable raising my hands, and the person beside me can feel comfortable not raising his/her hands." He wanted the freedom to worship as God led, and he wanted others to have that same freedom. As you grow in worship, you will find that freedom.

Your Daily Walk

Scripture:

Romans 12:1-2 is your first memory passage of Week 9. Detach the card from the back of the book, review the scripture, place it with your other memory flash cards and spend priority time today reviewing and memorizing them all.

Application:

What has changed as I am growing in worship? _____

_____

Journal: _____

_____

_____

_____

_____

_____

_____

_____

_____

_____

_____

_____

_____

_____

_____

_____

_____

_____

Prayer: _____

_____

_____

_____

_____

_____

_____

_____

_____

Know Whom You Worship

He is Lord

"He is Lord, He is Lord, He is risen from the dead and He is Lord.
Every knee shall bow, every tongue confess, that Jesus Christ is Lord."[11]

I had sung the song "He is Lord" for over twenty years. As I began to grow in worship I began to change how I sang the song. I began singing:

You are Lord, You are Lord, You are risen from the dead and You are Lord.
Every knee should bow, every tongue confess, that Jesus, You are Lord.

Why did I change the words. There were three realities that caused me to alter the way that I was singing this song. First, I recognized that this song and many others say something <u>about</u> God when they could just as easily be turned around to say something <u>to</u> God. The Psalmist says, *"Sing to the Lord a new song"* (Psalm 96:1; 149:1b; NIV). It is not wrong to sing songs about God. Moses and Miriam's songs in Exodus 15:1-18 and 21 are songs about God. However, both songs begin by encouraging people to sing <u>to</u> the Lord. Mary, Jesus' mother, sang a song to God and about God when He confirmed that she would be the mother of the Lord (Luke 1:46-55). The Bible does not say her words were a song, but the rhyme and meter would have been consistent with a song.

Singing songs about God can help encourage believers to remember what God has done, but if these are all we sing, then we can become prone to be disengaged as we sing. I have no doubt that many people are more comfortable being disengaged in worship. If our lives are not in tune with God, we will be more comfortable singing songs about Him instead of to Him. If our lives are in tune with God, we will turn songs about Him into songs sung to Him. If our lives are not in tune with God, and we are directed by the worship leader to sing songs to Him, then we are often convicted and directed to confess our sin and line up with Him.

The second realization that changed the way I sing "He is Lord" is my knowledge of scripture. The song "He is Lord" comes from Philippians 2:10-11. Paul says "...that at the name of Jesus every knee <u>should</u> bow," not shall bow. It is obvious that every time we hear the precious name of our Savior, we do not bow, but we should.

Some of the most powerful songs that are written are songs from the Bible. You may also notice that songs to God are, in reality, prayers. Therefore, when we sing songs from the Bible, then we are praying scripture set to music. In order for our scripture prayers to be powerful, it is important that the words we sing from the Bible be accurate.

Third, since I know that the Bible instructs me to sing to God, not just about Him, I began to focus my worship on the Father, not the song. I began to think of ways I could alter songs in my mind so that my worship would be both scripturally correct and spiritually motivated.

How have these realizations changed my worship? Worship is exciting. I look forward to gathering with believers to worship the Lord. I enjoy riding in my car worshiping the Lord. I like getting in small groups and worshiping the Lord. I am refreshed when I am on my knees in worship.

Begin to look for opportunities to sing to the Lord. You may want to sing about what He has done, but be certain to find ways to tell Him how you feel. It is God you and I are worshiping. He deserves our undivided attention and focused worship.

Your Daily Walk

Scripture:
    Colossians 3:16

Application:
    What is your favorite song? _____
What does that song say to God?_____
What does it says about God?_____

Journal: _____

_____
_____
_____
_____
_____
_____
_____
_____
_____
_____
_____
_____
_____
_____
_____
_____
_____

Prayer: _____

_____
_____
_____
_____
_____
_____
_____

How Much Will It Cost? Part 1

"All they do at church is talk about money." Have you ever heard this statement? It is always an exaggeration. Churches can, however, if they are not careful, spend an inordinate amount of time discussing money.

The purpose of Christian giving is not simply to meet budgets and provide buildings. Biblical giving is another sign of a Christian's growth.

1. When Christians give, they demonstrate that they believe that God owns it all. The Psalmist David said that God owns the cattle on a thousand hills (Psalm 50:10). He also owns the hills. Psalm 24:1 says, *"The earth is the Lord's, and everything in it, the world, and all who live in it"* (NIV).

God tells Christians to return the tithe to Him, and He will return to us what we need (Malachi 3:7-12). What is a tithe? Genesis 14 records God blessing a man called Abram. God gave Abram victory in battle, and Abram recovered his nephew Lot and the goods that were stolen. Then Abram gave God a tenth of all he had. God followed by making a covenant with Abram. He promised to make Abram the father of many nations and He changed his name to Abraham which means "father of many."

Notice the sequence. (1) God chose Abram. (2) Abram fought for what was right. (3) God blessed Abram. (4) Abram gave God the tenth. (5) God made the new man, Abraham, a wealthy blessing to many nations.

Do you know what God wants to do in the believer's life? (1) God has chosen Christians. (2) Christians should stand for righteousness. (3) God will bless us. (4) We give. (5) God makes us a blessing to others.

2. When Christians give, they demonstrate obedience. Jesus endorsed tithing in Matthew 23:23b. *"For you pay tithe of mint and anise and cummin, and have neglected the weightier matters of the law: justice and mercy and faith. These you ought to have done, without leaving the others undone."* Giving at least 10 percent of our resources is similar to giving one seventh of our days. God, in Exodus 20:8 tells us to set one day aside for Him. God does not want one day; He wants all seven. When we give God one day, we are saying that He has all our days. God does not want a tenth, half or even three-fourths of our resources. He wants us to know that it is all His. When we return the tithe, we are saying that we believe He owns it all, and we want to obey Him.

Conversely, when we will not set aside a day or a tithe, then we are saying that God does not control our time and money.

Let me pause to move outside the realm of legalism. I often talk about tithing (the tenth) because I have discovered that most Christians who have no place to start do little or nothing. There is a more excellent way. Learn how to give from the heart. Paul in 2 Corinthians 9:7 says, *"Each man should give what he has decided in his heart to give, not reluctantly or under compulsion, for God loves a cheerful giver" (NIV).* Before you believe this is a license to give less, go back and read 2 Corinthians 9:6. *"Remember this: Whoever sows sparingly will also reap sparingly, and whoever sows generously will also reap generously."* Now read 2 Corinthians 9:8, *"And God is able to make all grace abound to you, so that in all things at all times, having all that you need, you will abound in every good work."* Be careful not to be stingy with the "owner." Remember, He has all the resources you will ever need.

    3.   When Christians give, it is worship. (*to be continued tomorrow*)

Your Daily Walk

Scripture:
    2 Corinthians 9:6-8

Memory verse: Remove the card that says "2 Corinthians 9:6" from your "To Learn" group and move it to your "Working to Memorize" group. Verse 6 is your second memory verse of Week 9.

Application:
    Give something this week as an act of worship. Pray that God will guide you to be obedient to tithe and to go beyond the tithe and trust Him with offerings.

Journal: _____

_____

_____

_____

_____

_____

_____

_____

_____

_____

_____

_____

_____

_____

_____

_____

_____

Prayer: _____

_____

_____

_____

_____

_____

_____

How Much Will It Cost? Part 2

Week 9, Day 5 - Thursday - Date: _____/_____/_____

Christian giving grows as we grow as disciples. Yesterday, we learned that returning a portion of our resources to God demonstrates trust and obedience. Continued from Day 4: *3. When Christians give, it is worship.* Many new believers (and even older ones) want to know how much it will cost. Returning a portion of our resources to God is another step in the life of a growing disciple. When Christians give out of love and trust and not out of compulsion or coercion, they soon discover that it does not cost; it pays. Abram gave as an act of worship, and he discovered that he could not out give God. God will never be in debt to His children.

Christians do not give because of what we will get, but because of what we have already received, the priceless gift of salvation. Giving is a humble overflow from our grateful hearts. It is worship.

We often receive an offering after communion. It is generally a token gift that everyone gives after we recognize that Jesus gave <u>all</u> He had on the Cross. After a 2004 observance of the Lord's Supper, a friend of mine explained that an orphanage in Moldova needed a new heating system. Children had frozen to death in the orphanage in previous years. As an act of worship, people gave generously and abundantly to meet half the immediate need. Most of what people gave was beyond the minimum requirement. We call this an offering.

God wants us to regularly return to Him a portion of what we have received. Periodically, He will lead us to return an offering. We do not give because God needs our money. You will recall that He is the owner. He owns everything we possess. He has lent to us the goods and resources we have and the world in which we live. One day we will be gone, and He will remain. He will take all we have and pass it on to someone else. Even if we have it hidden, it is His, and He knows where it is. Nothing we have is secure and nothing we "own" will last forever.

When I first became a Christian, I learned the importance of tithing and was obedient to do so. I then heard a number of messages that made me afraid not to tithe. As I grew, and long after I began preaching, I recognized that God wanted me to love Him enough to trust Him. I learned that giving the tithe was secondary. Telling God I believed that He owned it all and could meet more of my needs with 90 percent of my resources than I could with 100 percent was primary. It was at that time that my wife, Karen, and I began to increase the percentage of our tithe. We began to give offerings that were beyond anything we had ever done. In the process, she became a stay-at-home mom, and God continued to bless our lives and meet our needs.

We give to tell God that we love Him, trust Him and honor Him. He receives what we give, multiplies it and returns it to us. Paul says, *"God loves a cheerful giver"* (2 Corinthians 9:7, NIV). The word "cheerful" is from the Greek word, *hilaron.* This verse literally translates, *"God loves a hilarious giver"* (LPP). Most believers miss the blessings of cheerful generosity. I encourage you to join the growing number of God's trustworthy managers.

In 1 Corinthians 4:2, the Bible calls Christian "stewards." A steward is a manager. One thing I know about managers is that, if they are dishonest, they can lose their jobs. The corporate scandals of the 1990's and early 21st Century demonstrated that managers who seek selfish gain and steal will be punished. God has given us His world to manage. He requires one thing according to 1 Corinthians 4:2. He requires that we be "faithful managers." Faithful giving comes from faithful managers who are faithful worshipers.

Your Daily Walk

Scripture:
1 Corinthians 4:2

Application:
Become a faithful manager for God. If you have not given a tithe or offering as an act of worship, do so this Sunday. The Bible says *"Test me in this,"* says *the LORD Almighty, "and see if I will not throw open the floodgates of heaven and pour out so much blessing that you will not have room enough for it"* (Malachi 3:10, NIV).

Journal: _____

_____

_____

_____

_____

_____

_____

_____

_____

_____

_____

_____

_____

_____

_____

Prayer: _____

_____

_____

_____

_____

_____

_____

Clean Up Before You Eat
Week 9, Day 6 - Friday - Date: _____/_____/_____

Yesterday you read about a special offering that followed communion. You may have wondered what communion is. Communion is another important part of worship. Many new believers become anxious when they experience their first communion. Communion is also referred to as the Lord's Supper and the Eucharist. (Eucharist from the Greek *eucharistos* = to give thanks). [Matthew 26:17-30; Luke 22:7-23; Mark 14:12-21; 1 Corinthians 11:17-32] All are correct descriptions. The Bible says that on the night Jesus was betrayed, He gathered with His disciples to eat supper which was communion. While they were eating, Jesus used bread and drink for a special addition to the meal (the Lord's Supper). Before He broke the bread or distributed the cup, He gave thanks.

Observing the Lord's Supper should be a blessed time and a cautious time. It is a blessed time because the one who takes communion is identifying with the life, death and resurrection of Jesus. It is a cautious time because God's word teaches the importance of being clean before eating the bread and drinking the cup. There are four important parts to communion.

1. Confession - Today's session is entitled "Clean Up Before You Eat." Paul records in 1 Corinthians 11:30 that people who were participating in communion were getting sick, and some were dying. He says they were unworthy when they ate the Lord's Supper.

Sin in our lives would make us unworthy. The believer needs to confess all sin before participating in the Eucharist. Taking communion is a serious act of worship. Do not be flippant or take this time lightly. The Father is interested in our reverently observing the life and death of His Son.

2. The Bread - The bread and the cup are often called "the elements" of communion. Jesus first took the bread. When observing the Lord's Supper, the pastor or leader of the worship time will often take the bread and remind the church that the bread represents the body that Christ gave. He will give thanks and give the bread to the believers, have others distribute the bread, or ask the participants to come to a table or an altar. The leader will then instruct the congregation to eat the bread.

It is important to note that Jesus said the bread represents a body that was broken for us. Yet the Bible teaches that not one bone was broken, on the Cross (John 19:31-33). When Jesus talked about His body being broken, He may not have been talking about His physical body. The part of Him that was broken was much more serious and painful than the physical. When Jesus took our sin on Himself on the Cross, He was breaking His relationship with the Father and Holy Spirit. The Bible says that God's *"...eyes are too pure to look on evil; He cannot tolerate wrong"* (Habakkuk 1:13, NIV). When Jesus took on our sin, He felt forsaken by a Father who is so Holy that He cannot view sin.

3. The Cup - The cup, usually grape juice, represents the blood of Jesus.

The Bible says that His blood cleanses us from our sin (Ephesians 1:7). *"Without the shedding of blood there is no forgiveness"* (Hebrews 9:22, NIV). I often tell new believers to keep their first communion cup if the church uses individual disposable cups. This cup helps them remember the price Jesus paid for their salvation.

4. The Song - The Bible says that after the supper, they sang and departed to pray. Strive to leave communion worship with a praise song on your lips from a life that is open to listening to God.

Observing the Lord's Supper is an important time of worship. It is a holy time.

Your Daily Walk

Scripture:

John 19:31-33

Application:

Give thanks to Jesus for giving His life for you. Try to discover when your church will be having Communion worship. Before your next communion, return to page 131-132 and prepare your life for a powerful experience.

Journal: _____

_____
_____
_____
_____
_____
_____
_____
_____
_____
_____
_____
_____
_____
_____
_____
_____

Prayer: _____

_____
_____
_____
_____
_____
_____
_____
_____

A Time to Reflect, Recover and Review
Week 9, Day 7 - Saturday - Date: ____/____/_____

Today is the day to enhance your growth as a disciple. Review the week. Reflect on new material you have learned and insights you have underlined or highlighted. Return and read any material that you may have neglected to read and make journal entries on the days where you did not complete the assignments.

Let today be a day of spiritual recovery and reflection. Strive to meet with a discipler who can answer questions you may have and provide insights from what you have read. If you have done each day's assignment as designed, then enjoy this time of rest and review. Remember each day is important. Every study is designed to build on the foundation, Jesus, and construct the seven pillars of a Christian's faith: Prayer, Worship, Witness, Bible Study, Discipleship, Fellowship and Service.

Take time to be certain you have learned the two memory verses for this week and review the memory verses from the previous weeks.

Highlights from Week 9:
Read through each day of Week 9 and record a teaching from each day:
- Monday   - _____
_____
- Tuesday   - _____
_____
- Wednesday- _____
_____
- Thursday   - _____
_____
- Friday   - _____
_____

Journal:
Take time to write in your journal. Write down ideas and record events that are impacting your life in Christ. Record the victories and the struggles, the concepts you are learning and those you still do not understand.

_____
_____
_____
_____
_____
_____

Prayer: Talk to God today. Listen to what He is saying to you.
Remember: Tomorrow is the traditional day to worship God. Whether your worship time is Friday night, Saturday or Sunday, ask God to help you to prepare before worship. Do not wait until your day of worship to rest and get ready. Prepare in advance so that you will get the most from worship.

Week 10

Psalm 119:105 Your word is a lamp to my feet & a light for my path.

Ps 119:105

Build your Confidence

Question 1: How many bites from the fruit of the tree of the knowledge of good and evil did it take to separate Adam from God? Maybe you do not think the Bible tells us. It does. In Romans 5:16 the Bible says, "After Adam sinned once, he was judged guilty."

Question 2: Why did God stop the building of the Tower of Babel? Did He? The Bible says that when God confused the language of the people, they stopped the building of "the city" (Genesis 11:8).

Question 3: How far along was Elizabeth in her pregnancy when Mary visited her? Answer: Six months. How long did Mary stay with her? Answer: Three months. Did Mary wait until the birth of John the Baptist before returning to tell Joseph the news? What did Jesus say in Matthew 28:20? a. Teach them to obey? or b. Teach them to obey everything I said? Answer: b. Bible teaching should begin with the commands of Christ.

How did you do on these questions? Trust me, most teachers and some pastors would not do well. We often read the Bible with preconceptions given to us by cute stories and magnetic movies instead of reading what it actually says. We must learn how to hear from God and how to become confident in the Bible, the word of God.

While the third pillar of a Christian's life is Witness, we will save the discussion of pillar three until week twelve. Today's sequence in the Sunday School edition of *More Abundant LIFE* takes us, appropriately I believe, to **Bible Study**. Week 10 will help the reader to understand why he/she needs to get to know God through His word, the Bible. The more we get to know God, the more we trust Him. The more we trust Him, the more we obey and serve Him.

Be Committed to Worship
Week 10, Day 1 - Sunday - Date: _____/_____/_____

Week 10 will guide the believer to understand the importance of studying the Bible. Have you found a Sunday Bible study group? Most churches offer small group Bible studies. Find time to honor God by learning about Him. Find a place where Christians are encouraged to study His word.

Take your copy of *More Abundant LIFE* to worship and Bible study and take notes. The more you write, the more you will retain.

Worship includes giving and receiving. Pay attention to what you do in worship today. The Bible says, *"Therefore by Him let us continually **offer the sacrifice of praise** to God, that is, the fruit of our lips, giving thanks to His name."* (Hebrews 13:15, NKJ) Ask yourself these questions:

1. Did I give anything to God in worship today? ___Yes ___No
2. Did I offer an acceptable sacrifice of praise? ___Yes ___No
3. What did I receive from God? _____

The title of the pastor's message:_____
The main Bible text:_____
The main points of the pastor's message: _____
_____
_____
_____
_____
_____
_____
_____
_____
_____
This is what I learned that I can apply to my life: _____
_____
_____

Prayer: "Lord, help me to apply your word to my life and help me to be faithful each day this week to learn how to be strengthened in my faith by learning about you." Now ask God to help you apply what you have learned today. _____
_____
_____
_____
_____
_____
_____

What's In It for Me?

New believers often wonder if the Bible is relevant. How can a book that was completed over nineteen hundred years ago help me? The worth of the Bible is partially derived from the reality that it does not need periodic revisions. Paul's letter to Timothy explains that the Bible is inspired by God. *"All Scripture is God-breathed and is useful for teaching, rebuking, correcting and training in righteousness"* (2 Timothy 3:16, NIV). The word "inspired" is a translation from two Greek words *Theo pneustos (p* is silent). *Theo* means God and *pneustos* translates as "breathed." The Bible was written by men who were led by God's Spirit. They were literally led by God's "breath."

The believer's salvation is evidence of the Bible's relevance. Each twenty-first century believer is a member of the Kingdom of God because of his/her faith. Hebrews 11 uses the word "faith" twenty-seven times to describe why God blessed the lives of the heroes of the Old Testament who lived and died before Christ (B.C.). The faith of today's believer is in Jesus, while their faith was perfected by the coming of Jesus. From Abel (Hebrews 11:4; Genesis 4:4) to the present age, salvation has been through faith. Paul in Ephesians 2:8 says, *"By grace you have been saved —through faith— and this not from yourselves; it is the gift of God..."* (NIV)

We believe Jesus' words are true. We must believe that all His teachings are relevant. To live by the Bible, one must understand the relevance of the Bible to our lives today. *More Abundant LIFE* shows how Jesus taught us to (1) pray (Matthew 6). He also taught us to (2) worship. From His baptism to the cross, He taught us how to worship. He taught us to (3) witness. From His first command (Matthew 4:19) to His last command (Acts 1:8), Jesus told us to witness, and through His life-style He taught us to witness. He taught the (4) Bible. He taught us the importance of learning the Bible by often quoting scripture. He told us and showed us how to make (5) disciples (Matthew 28:19). The goal of this book is to help you become a growing disciple. Jesus enjoyed (6) fellowship. His first miracle was performed at a wedding ceremony. He told us that He, the Son of God, came to (7) serve (Matthew 20:28). If He is to serve, then we are to serve.

The above paragraph demonstrates how Jesus worked to strengthen all seven pillars that MAL promotes. The Bible teaches us all that we, the believers, need to know about these seven pillars of our faith. However, the words of the Bible are of no value unless we read, study and apply these words to our individual Christian lives. *More Abundant LIFE* is designed to help the reader both discover what the Bible says about these pillars and to set the seven pillars of spiritual strength in place in a new believer's life.

As you read the Bible, you will discover that it will teach you how to live. The Bible will help correct your mistakes. It will provide training as you grow and serve. It will be relevant in your home life, business life, recreation life, church life, and all other parts of your life. There is much in the Bible for you. The Bible will instruct you and inspire you. However, the Bible cannot help you if it is closed and neglected. Open your Bible and discover what is in it for you.

Nine weeks ago you were challenged to begin to memorize verses from the Bible. Each week you have been provided with two more verses to read and to memorize. If the Bible is going to properly guide lives, it needs to be read and then learned. To have the Bible at our disposal twenty-four hours a day, seven days a week, no matter where we are in the world, it must be memorized. It is helpful to learn what the Bible says to know the essence of scripture, but it is powerful when the believer knows the exact words from the Bible.

Your Daily Walk

Scripture:
    2 Timothy 3:16

Memory verse: Remove the card that says "2 Timothy 3:16" from your "To Learn" group and move it to your "Working to Memorize" group. Know that God has a great plan for your life.

Application:
    Read a passage in the Bible today that is especially meaningful to you.

Journal: _____

_____

_____

_____

_____

_____

_____

_____

_____

_____

_____

_____

_____

_____

_____

_____

_____

Prayer: _____

_____

_____

_____

_____

_____

We Need More Salt!

An important part of Jesus' ministry is the Sermon on the Mount. This message can be found in Matthew's gospel, Chapters 5-7. The next four days will be spent on four of the most significant parts of this sermon. We need to know why it is necessary to study the Bible, but we also need to examine some of Jesus' teachings that demonstrate the relevance of the Bible for today's Christian.

The Christian as Salt

"You are the salt of the earth. But if the salt loses its saltiness, how can it be made salty again? It is no longer good for anything, except to be thrown out and trampled by men" (Matthew 5:13, NIV). You may not have known that Jesus called you salt, but He did. You are His salt in this world. Historically, salt has been used in a variety of ways. One important use of salt in the world where Jesus lived was as a preservative. Very few people had the means to send servants to the mountains to mine ice and return that ice to holes in the ground for a refrigeration system. Most people preserved meats, especially fish, by placing a layer of fish and then a layer of salt. Christians are kept in the world to be preservers of the words and work of Christ. We preserve the words of Christ by learning and then sharing them with others. We preserve the works of Christ by doing what He did and exemplifying His love. As you learn and speak words from the Bible, you are preserving the word of God.

In 1968, the *U.S.S. Pueblo* was captured by North Korea. Their crew was imprisoned. Stories from their capture revealed that while in prison they had been able to recreate a large portion of the Bible because of the collective knowledge of many of the crew. We are to learn the word of God so that we can preserve it in our speech and lives.

Another important use of salt is that it creates thirst. As we speak the word of God, it creates a thirst for Christ among the lost. You may have heard the saying, "You can lead a horse to water, but you can't make him drink." You can make him drink if you put enough salt on his tongue. That is why salt blocks are placed around horses. It is likely that whoever told you about Jesus shared many verses from the Bible, just as I did in Week 1, Day 4. No one could make you become a Christian, but the word of God provides the thirst that makes people want to come to Christ. It is more important that people hear Jesus' words than our words.

A third use of salt is to improve the taste of food. Christians should improve life around them. Others should know that we serve a risen Savior; we are excited about our faith, and have an unexplainable joy. If we improve life around us, then others will want to have that life we enjoy in Jesus.

A fourth use of salt is to destroy weeds. Salt, when it is not diluted, will get rid of weeds that Jesus says can stop our spiritual growth. He says that our weeds are the *"cares of this world and the deceitfulness of riches"* (Matthew 13:7; 22).

A fifth use of salt is to melt ice. When I lived in Kentucky, I used salt in the winter months to melt ice on walkways and driveways. Many non-believers are cold toward Christ and the Bible. The word of God melts cold hearts.

The Problem with Salt

Salt that is mixed with impurities is virtually useless. When salt is impure, its preserving power is weakened, its thirst-giving power reduced, its ability to enhance taste or control weeds is diminished, and its strength to melt ice is hindered. We must strive to keep our lives clean so that our "saltiness" will not be reduced, diminished, or hindered. Otherwise you and I, like the salt the first century fishermen used, will be good for nothing except to be thrown out on a dirt road to reduce the dust.

Your Daily Walk

Scripture:

Matthew 5:13

Memory verse: Remove the card that says "Matthew 5:13" from your "To Learn" group and move it to your "Working to Memorize" group. It is a simple but profound verse that will always be worth carrying in your head and heart.

Application:

Are you preserving the word of God? You can answer this question by answering the next question: "Are you faithfully striving to memorize the verses from each week." Memorizing scripture is an important step to preserving the Bible in our minds.

Journal: _____

_____
_____
_____
_____
_____
_____
_____
_____
_____
_____
_____
_____
_____

Prayer: _____

_____
_____
_____
_____
_____

Find Your Treasure

Week 10, Day 4 - Wednesday - Date: _____/_____/_____

"Do not store up for yourselves treasures on earth, where moth and rust destroy, and where thieves break in and steal. But store up for yourselves treasures in heaven, where moth and rust do not destroy, and where thieves do not break in and steal. For where your treasure is, there your heart will be also" (Matthew 6:19-21, NIV).

The businessmen stood and stared as their partner's body was lowered into its grave. "How much did he leave?" One asked. "Every dime," came the reply.

What legacy will you leave when you depart this life? Many Christians spend most of their lives preparing to leave businesses, houses, land, money, and yes, headaches to their children. Jesus said that the treasures of this world are subject to disintegrating, tarnishing and being stolen.

There are two products that will last eternally. These are (1) the word of God, the Bible, and (2) the souls of men, women, boys and girls. Given the choice of investing in what you know will disappear and what you know will last, which one will you choose? Chapter fourteen will explain the importance of helping people have eternal life. Today's goal is to help you to understand the importance of investing in the word of God and the work of Christ.

We are Managers

Last week the Christian's need to give financially to the work of the Kingdom of God was discussed. Paul, in 1 Corinthians 4:2 explains that we are managers. Some Bibles use the word stewards. The NIV says we have been given a trust, and we are to be faithful with the things God has entrusted to us.

A wealthy businessman had placed a large sum of money in a trust to help ministers and missionaries. A Christian leader would often help him find the best places to put the money and get it to those who needed it. He never sought to take anything from the businessman and demonstrated joy over every gift that was given. The businessman saw his heart, his love for helping, his faithfulness to properly distribute the resources and the absence of greed. His family's will named the Christian as the recipient of their millions with this statement from the businessman: "You have demonstrated that you know how God wants these resources used. I am leaving them to you for you to continue to distribute as God leads."

The Christian leader had been a faithful manager, and he was entrusted with even more to manage. Jesus, in Matthew 25:21, provided an illustration that demonstrates that those who are faithful managers will be given more to manage.

Christians have been given much more than a treasure of things. God has made us managers of His word. We are to read it, memorize it and share it. He has also made us managers of God-given abilities. We are to serve in such a way that we bring glory to Him. The Bible tells us to do whatever we do for the glory of God (1 Corinthians 10:31).

God has placed treasures in you that only you can manage and share. As you work to achieve in this world and survive this life, be certain to invest in something that will make it to the next life. As you study His word, you will discover real treasures that will make an eternal difference.

When my wife and I filed our "Last Will and Testament", we set aside an amount to give to the church when we die. I have often made the statement that I did not want to explain to Jesus, the first one I see after I die, why Karen and I left Him out of our Will. However, what we leave financially should be only a token of what we leave spiritually. We both want to leave more than things. We want to leave children and friends who know Christ and are growing in Christ. What treasure will you leave?

Your Daily Walk

Scripture:
Matthew 6:19-21

Application:
Notice in verse 21 that Jesus says *"For where your treasure is, there your heart will be also."* He does not say that we should get our hearts right and then our treasures will be in the right place. He teaches us that our heart "follows" our treasures. The more we invest our lives and resources in the Kingdom of God, the more our hearts will be connected to His work.

Leave a treasure that is worthy of Christ.

Journal: _____

_____

_____

_____

_____

_____

_____

_____

_____

_____

_____

_____

_____

_____

_____

_____

Prayer: _____

_____

_____

_____

_____

_____

Check the Roots

Week 10, Day 5 - Thursday - Date: _____/_____/_____

"By their fruit you will recognize them."

(Matthew 7:16a, NIV)

You may have heard people say that the Bible says not to judge. They are correct. We are not given the responsibility to condemn people to a Christless eternity or to award an individual eternal life in heaven. However, while Jesus did tell us not to judge, He called us to be fruit inspectors. Jesus told us in Matthew 7:15 to be on the alert for teachers who might lead us astray. Then He tells us that we will know who are the followers and who are the fakes by the fruit in their lives. A great challenge that every new believer encounters is the challenge to know whom to believe. With so many ideas about what the Bible says and what Christians should do, how can you know whom to believe and whom to follow? Here are some questions that may help you check out who is teaching the truth.

1.   Is what you are being taught consistent with the Bible? You can be confident that God will never tell a twenty-first century teacher to say something that is contrary to the Bible. If you are not sure if a teacher is correctly interpreting a part of scripture, then see what a reputable commentary says. The most time honored English commentary is Matthew Henry's. It can be ordered through most bookstores, especially Christian stores. It is also readily available on the internet. The commentary is not always easy to read, but it is reliable.

2.   Is the life of the teacher one that is lived consistent with the teachings of the Bible? Are they winning people to Jesus? There are false teachers who will loudly proclaim what you and I should do while ignoring their own teachings and indulge in sinful activities that destroy a Christian's witness. Several years ago, I was told of a preacher who often preached on giving. When it was discovered that he did not give, he explained that he was already making sacrifices and did not need to give. He was wrong! The Bible has numerous passages that challenge God's ministers to give and even be leaders in giving.

A criticism of modern politicians is that they often make laws for us that do not apply to them. God did not make one set of laws for leaders and another set for followers. His words that guide our lives are to be applied to everyone. When I see teachers of the Bible whose lives have bad fruit, I have to wonder in what they are rooted. They seem to be rooted in the world, not the word.

3.   What is God saying in my spirit? You are growing as a disciple. It is time that you learn to listen to God's Spirit. He does all the teaching. Jesus said in John 14:25-26, *"These things I have spoken to you while being present with you. But the Helper, the Holy Spirit, whom the Father will send in My name, He will teach you all things, and bring to your remembrance all things that I said to you"* (NKJ). When you are walking with Jesus, and you get an uneasy feeling about what you are learning, check it out! God's Spirit may be speaking to your mind.

You and I need to produce good fruit. The good fruit that we produce will come from the Holy Spirit inside of us. Let us be certain that we are becoming rooted in the principles of the Bible so that we can know how the Holy Spirit wants to guide us and to work through us. When challenged to do something contrary to the Spirit and His word, we must resist the temptation to sin and seek to follow the Savior. Remember good roots equal good fruit.

Caution: Be very careful that you are walking with Jesus when you get feelings that something may be wrong with what you are hearing. The enemy, the devil, will speak to a mind not tuned into the Father. The Bible says he can appear as an angel of light. Some people are not totally walking with Jesus and they get this "feeling" and think it is from God, but it is not.

Three Bible study teachers were gossiping about the preacher and his leadership. This had gone on for so long that they did not recognize that they were engaged in unconfessed sin. One day these teachers left the church. They explained that they did not "feel" the pastor was teaching truth. When confronted with their statements, they could not give one example. Their feelings came from an enemy who took advantage of their simple, gossiping ways. They were wrong, but the enemy made them believe everyone else was wrong.

A man left home early one morning. His wife called. "Honey, are you OK?" "Fine", he said. "It just came on the radio that someone is driving the wrong way on the interstate", she warned. "Someone", he replied, "there are hundreds going the wrong way." Does this sound familiar? Sometimes we are so in error that we do not understand that the collision that is coming is because we are wrong.

Your Daily Walk

Scripture:

John 14:25-26

Application:

Pray today for the Godly teachers and/or preachers who are helping or will help you to grow as a Christian. Pray that you will be able to discern false teachers who either do not correctly teach how to apply scripture, or fail to apply to their lives what they are teaching.

Journal: _____

_____

_____

_____

_____

_____

_____

_____

Prayer: _____

_____

_____

_____

Don't Build on the Beach

"Therefore everyone who hears these words of mine and puts them into practice is like a wise man who built his house on the rock. The rain came down, the streams rose, and the winds blew and beat against that house; yet it did not fall because it had its foundation on the rock. But everyone who hears these words of mine and does not put them into practice is like a foolish man who built his house on sand. The rain came down, the streams rose, and the winds blew and beat against that house, and it fell with a great crash" (Matthew 7:24-27, NIV).

Building your Christian life through Bible study requires that you both read and apply to your life the words that you read. Jesus in Matthew 7:24-27 describes two people. Both were house builders, but only one house survived. Today you will learn how to be a success or failure in your Christian walk.

Read the Word

Every serious believer is going to spend time studying the Bible. The wise believer reads the Bible and seeks to apply the teachings of scripture to his/her life. The foolish believer will read and even listen to others teach, but he/she will not consistently apply the Bible to his/her daily life. The unbeliever will hardly, if ever, read the Bible and can only apply the teachings of salvation to his/her life.

As a believer you are encouraged to read the word of God so that you can hear God speak to you. Proverbs 9:10 says *"The fear of the Lord is the beginning of wisdom, and the knowledge of the Holy One is understanding"* (NKJ). To fear God is to revere God. To revere Him is to respect and honor Him above anyone and anything in the universe. This verse in Proverbs then goes on to say that "knowledge of the Holy One" (studying the Bible) will help you have "understanding" about how to fear (revere) Him. If you want to hear God, then read the word!

Watch for Storms

I entered scouting when I was eleven years old and received instructions on camping. I was taught to pitch my tent in the woods on high ground, but never in the sand or by a creek. One of my early camping tirps was to an area where the woods were rocky and the ground uneven. However, there was a creek with a sandy beach. We looked at the sky, and it was clear. We proceeded to pitch our tents on the soft, comfortable sand while our scoutmaster drove his tent pegs into rocky soil on uneven ground.

About three o'clock in the morning it began to rain and we learned that he was wise and we were foolish. I have enjoyed hundreds of days and nights of camping since that 1966 experience, but I have never pitched a tent in the sand again, and I still remember the consequences of not applying what I learned. The rain softened the sand and loosened the tent pegs, causing our tents to collapse. The creek rose, causing our sleeping bags and packs to get soaked. The rain then drenched all of us.

Wise and foolish students will experience trials which are the storms of life. Jesus said that when the wise students experience storms, they stand strong. Those who have a relationship with Him, know His word, and seek to apply His word survive the troubles and tragedies of life.

The foolish students read the word, but the "sky looks clear." They do not see immediate problems; therefore, they postpone application. It is incredible how quickly one's peaceful, sheltered life can turn to turmoil. What does the foolish builder do when trials come? Jesus said that their lives fall apart.

Bible study cannot be limited to a Sunday activity in which the Christian feels obligated to participate. It must become a daily quest for knowing God and then becoming like Jesus. The trials make us stronger and shine as a witness to the world that Jesus lives in us.

Your Daily Walk

Scripture:
Matthew 7:24-27
Application:
When did you read your Bible today? _____
Journal: _____

_____
_____
_____
_____
_____
_____
_____
_____
_____
_____
_____
_____
_____
_____
_____
_____

Prayer: _____

_____
_____
_____
_____
_____

A Time to Reflect, Recover and Review
Week 10, Day 7 - Saturday - Date: ____/____/_____

Saturday is the day to enhance your growth as a disciple. Review the week. Reflect on new material you have learned and insights you have underlined or highlighted. Return and read any material to and make journal entries on the days where you did not complete the assignments.

Let today be a day of spiritual recovery and reflection. Strive to meet with a discipler who can answer questions you may have and provide insights from what you have read. If you have done each day's assignment as designed, then enjoy this time of rest and review. Remember each day is important. Every study is designed to build on the foundation, Jesus, and construct the seven pillars of a Christian's faith: Prayer, Worship, Witness, Bible Study, Discipleship, Fellowship and Service.

Take time to be certain you have learned the two memory verses for this week and review the memory verses from the previous weeks.

Highlights from Week 10:
Read through each day of Week 10 and record a teaching from each day:
- Monday   - _____

- Tuesday   - _____

- Wednesday- _____

- Thursday - _____

- Friday   - _____

Journal:
Take time to write in your journal. Write down ideas and record events that are impacting your life in Christ. Record the victories and the struggles, the concepts you are learning and those you still do not understand.

_____
_____
_____
_____
_____

Prayer: Talk to God today. Listen to what He is saying to you.
Remember: Tomorrow is the traditional day to worship God. Whether your worship time is Friday night, Saturday or Sunday, ask God to help you to prepare before worship. Do not wait until your day of worship to rest and get ready. Prepare in advance so that you will get the most from worship.

Week 11

Build your Christian Character

Exodus 19:24 records an often overlooked command of God to Moses. God tells Moses to go down and get his brother Aaron and bring him to the mountain with him. Moses goes down, receives the Ten Commandments, is confronted by a nation afraid of the voice of God and goes back up Mt. Sinai to get the rest of the law. Unfortunately, he forgot one important matter. He forgot to bring Aaron with him. Exodus 32 records the people of God building a golden calf. The leader was none other than Aaron, the man who was supposed to be on the mountain with Moses. There was another time when Aaron went up Mt. Sinai, but Moses did not take him and he did not stay.

How many golden calves are being built in our communities because believers do not want to take the time to bring less mature believers to the mountain with them? Jesus, in Matthew 28:19, tells us to "make disciples," not just decisions.

The fifth pillar of a Christian's life is **Discipleship**. Week 11 teaches those who are growing through *More Abundant LIFE* why it is important to apply what you are learning from the Bible. The goal is to become a disciple who looks like Jesus. Jesus said for us to follow Him. That is the essence of discipleship. He also commanded us to disciple others. Isn't it time to do the Master's business?

Be Committed to Worship

Week 11, Day 1 - Sunday - Date: _____/_____/_____

Sunday is a day of corporate worship. Most churches also offer small group Bible studies. Find time to honor God. Find a place where Christians are encouraged to worship, and the lost are invited to come to Christ.

Take your copy of *More Abundant LIFE* and take notes. The more you write, the more you will retain.

Worship includes giving and receiving. Pay attention to what you do in worship today. The Bible says, *"Therefore by Him let us continually **offer the sacrifice of praise** to God, that is, the fruit of our lips, giving thanks to His name."* (Hebrews 13:15, NKJ) Ask yourself these questions:

1. Did I give anything to God in worship today?   ___Yes ___No
2. Did I offer an acceptable sacrifice of praise?   ___Yes ___No
3. What did I receive from God? _____

The title of the pastor's message:_____
The main Bible text:_____
The main points of the pastor's message: _____

_____
_____
_____
_____
_____
_____
_____
_____
_____
_____
_____

This is what I learned that I can apply to my life: _____

_____
_____
_____

Prayer: "Lord, help me to apply your word to my life."

_____
_____
_____
_____

Grow Deep!

"Leaders must keep hold of the deep truths of the faith with a clear conscience. They must first be tested and if they are applying what they have learned, then let them serve as leaders" (1 Timothy 3:9-10, LPP). Many Christians make the mistake of equating Bible study and biblical knowledge with discipleship. I had a professor in college who knew the Bible better than most Christians I have met, yet claimed to be an atheist. Knowing what the Bible says does not necessarily translate into practice. Christian discipleship begins with studying the Bible. However, it goes beyond knowledge to putting into practice what we have learned. Then disciples must pass on to others what we both know and have applied. It is important to know the truths of the Bible, to apply those principles as we learn them and then to teach them to others in such a way that they can apply those same principles.

The two verses at the top of the page come from the Apostle Paul who, in his first letter to Timothy, instructed Timothy to give those who wanted to be leaders an opportunity to be tested. Trials will teach the Christian how firmly he/she believes what he/she has been taught and/or is teaching. Surviving trials, tests and temptations teaches us that we do have a growing relationship with God through Jesus.

Storms have a way of exposing trees whose roots are shallow. Similarly if the Christian's roots are grounded only in knowledge, then his/her trials will create panic, worry, fear and even attempts to flee.

Jesus said that the poor in spirit will be blessed. I can read those words. I can understand that He is talking about people who humbly acknowledge they are nothing nor have anything outside of Christ. However, if we do not practice humility, then we will become prideful and take the glory that is due God. If we take credit when we are recognized or given an award for an accomplishment, then our "trial of success" will bring us down.

Did you see that spiritual curve ball I just threw you? Most of us believe trials come only in the form of negative experiences. God is teaching me that some of my greatest trials come from rewards and successes. The negative is often easy to recognize. Many Christian leaders teach us how to deal with the negative. We need more people to teach us how to deal with blessings. We need to learn how to respond when we win. The wisdom writer of Proverbs 27:21 says: *"... man is tested by the praise he receives."*

When you and I can apply God's word so that we can overcome problems and not be shaken by success, then we will know that we are growing into a deeper relationship with Him. Years ago, I met a man who was an advocate of personal discipleship. He consistently spoke of the need to have a deeper walk yet this same man worked behind the scenes to undermine his pastor's ministry and to thwart the forward motion of his church. We need to hear the truth of the Bible, but we must apply those truths to our lives. Be certain that your actions are not so negatively loud that others cannot hear what you are saying. We do not grow to know; we know to grow. Edification without application leads to stagnation. Deep water is seldom stagnate. Christians who grow deep are learning to apply the principles of the Bible.

Growing deep will not be easy. You will need to search the scriptures, and study on your own to get solid food from the word of God. Pray often and determine in your spirit that you can and will reach spiritual depths in your spiritual walk through Christ who will give you all the strength that you will need.

Your Daily Walk

Scripture:
1 Timothy 3:9-10
Application:
What did you apply in your life today that you have learned in the past?

_____

Journal: _____

_____
_____
_____
_____
_____
_____
_____
_____
_____
_____
_____
_____
_____
_____
_____

Prayer: _____

_____
_____
_____
_____

Grow Wide!
Week 11, Day 3 - Tuesday - Date: _____/_____/_____

The first week of *More Abundant LIFE* explained the importance of having a broad base to your spiritual life. A tall building with a narrow base will topple over. Look at this picture.

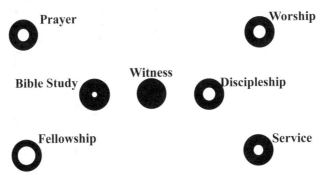

Allow the above circles to be the pillars that are supporting the building of my spiritual life. Each one is necessary or the building is going to topple over. The one in the center is the most important, but all are necessary.

In my life, sharing my faith (being a witness) and discipling others to do so are my greatest passions. However, without the other six pillars my life will become unbalanced.

Below, are seven pillars. I want you to do this exercise. Do you know what your passion is? Which of the seven columns interests you the most? Write that one over the center circle. Now label the other circles. Fill in the circles in proportion to how much you know about each one. If you know more about prayer than worship, color in more of that circle. Work on increasing your knowledge and practice of the circles that have more white space.

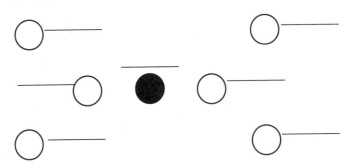

Matthew 23:23 records Jesus' commending the Pharisees for tithing. *"You tithe of your mint, dill and cummin...These you should have done..."* (KJV) He said. Then He admonished them for neglecting other teachings such as justice, mercy and faithfulness.

The Christian who balances the seven parts of his/her life will have the greatest potential for making a lasting impact on the world around him/her. You need to recall from the first week's teachings that the height of a building is directly related to the strength of the foundation and the width of the base. The foundation is Jesus. He is as strong and as wide a foundation as you will ever need. The width of your spiritual life will depend on how many strong spiritual pillars you have in place. The width of your spiritual life determines how far your influence will reach and how lasting your influence will be. Set a goal to grow wide so that your influence in this world will outlast your life.

Your Daily Walk

Scripture:
John 15:8

Memory verse: Remove the card that says "John 15:8" from your "To Learn" group and move it to your "Working to Memorize" group. John 15:8 is your first memory verse for this week and your twenty-first of this study. This verse will help you to know that your fruitful influence demonstrates to the world that you are Christ's disciple.

Application:
Work on a weak pillar today.

Journal: _____

_____

_____

_____

_____

_____

_____

_____

_____

_____

_____

_____

_____

_____

_____

_____

_____

Prayer: _____

_____

_____

_____

_____

Grow Up!

"Therefore, dear friends, since you already know this, be on your guard so that you may not be carried away by the error of lawless men and fall from your secure position. But grow in the grace and knowledge of our Lord and Savior Jesus Christ. To him be glory both now and forever!" (2 Peter 3:17-18, NIV).

Never become complacent about your growth as a Christian. Complacency leads to stagnation. A stagnate Christian is useless to God. Wherever you are in your spiritual walk, determine to keep growing.

Peter told us to be on our guard so that we do not succumb to wrong teachings. Paul told us to move beyond spiritual childhood. He encourages Christians to grow up so that they would not be subject to the latest spiritual side show that sounds good, but has little substance. Read his words.

"That we should no longer be children, tossed to and fro and carried about with every wind of doctrine, by the trickery of men, in the cunning craftiness of deceitful plotting" (Ephesians 4:14, NKJ).

There comes a time in a believer's life when he/she moves on toward maturity. What are signs of spiritual maturity?

1.   As you grow, you will get to the place in your spiritual walk where your desires will not be as important as God's. Many Christians in churches talk about themselves. They use phrases like "This is what I like..." or "I want to see us do..." or "I don't like..." or "When are we going to..." or "I think..." Periodically well meaning Christians will come to me and tell me that they think I should preach on a certain subject or passage. It is interesting to note that mature believers seldom give such advice. When mature believers provide suggestions about preaching or teaching they usually preface their suggestion by explaining that they were praying. They often conclude their words by encouraging me not to listen to them but to listen to God. Rick Warren's *Purpose Driven Life* is an excellent book that reminds believers that this life is not about us; it is about Him, our God.

2.   As you grow, you will become more uncomfortable with sin. Before accepting Christ you may have gone places with ungodly friends for the purpose of doing things that displease God. You may still go where those friends are, but now you will do so to reach them. However, you will not be comfortable staying there. You will hear about people dying and wonder where they are now. You will become sad at the things in this world and our nation that hurt God's heart.

3.   As you grow, you will argue less and pray more. You will listen to people who do not understand the word of God, but will respond to those who are less mature or lost with a spirit of love. You will not condescend, and you will want to help them to grow up. You will learn to pray for them when you see them or God brings them to your mind.

4.   Maybe the greatest sign of spiritual maturity is knowing that criticism does not hurt as much as it once did. When Jesus saved us, we were to crucify our

old nature. If criticism still hurts, you are just not dead enough yet. It will take years of spiritual growth before you deflect lies and criticisms without getting angry, depressed, or anxious.

I have noticed that when we are growing in Christ, the bumps in the road do not send us into a ditch. The disciples who attempt to represent maturity but have a false spirituality will not survive the struggles. Paul tries to teach these believers not to start over, but to start and then grow up.

We as Christians can grow deep in the word and our practice of the scriptures. We can become balanced and build a wide base that takes us to a lost world. Ultimately we must grow up. Without growing deeper and wider, we will not be able to grow up.

Your Daily Walk

Scripture:
2 Peter 3:17-18

Application:
List the seven pillars of growing a balanced Christian life.

1. P_____   4. B_____   7. S_____
2. W_____   5. D_____
3. W_____   6. F_____

Journal: _____

_____

_____

_____

_____

_____

_____

_____

_____

_____

_____

_____

_____

_____

_____

_____

_____

Prayer: _____

_____

_____

_____

_____

Grow Out!

Week 11, Day 5 - Thursday - Date: _____/_____/_____

"Therefore, as you go, make disciples of all nations, baptizing them in the name of the Father and of the Son and of the Holy Spirit" (Matthew 28:19, LPP).

Churches use the word *missions* to describe how disciples grow outwardly. There comes a time in our spiritual growth when believers grow to the place that their lives begin to influence and impact other nations. The words of Jesus, recorded in Matthew 28:19, tell us to make disciples of all nations. The Greek word for nations is *ethnos*. From *ethnos* we get the English word *ethnic*. The instruction of Jesus is much broader than reaching a recognized nation. Jesus calls us to reach all people groups. We are to reach every ethnic group.

Who are the ethnics? Paul only recognized two groups, the Jews and the ethnics. He called them Gentiles. If you are reading this book, then you are either a Jew or a Gentile. Your responsibility is to reach both the Jews and the Gentiles with the gospel of Jesus. Paul, in Romans 1:16, says, *"I am not ashamed of the gospel, because it is the power of God for the salvation of everyone who believes: first for the Jew, then for the Gentile"* (NIV). God sent His Son into the world so that everyone might be saved. Someone shared that news with us. We were saved, and now we must go to the world to share that news with others. Where will God send you?

God will send you to minister to hurting people in your community. There are needs and opportunities to meet those needs. I remember a young man whose mother was killed in a wreck as she drove to pick him up from school. Christians in the church ministered to him, saw him accept Christ and supported him as he grew and went to college.

God will send you to minister to people in your state. There are church buildings that need to be built. There are communities that need to be canvassed. There will be tragedies that you will respond to and provide help. When God calls, be prepared to go.

God will send you to hurting people in other states. After the bombing of the twin towers in New York in 2001, there were hundreds of people from our state who travelled to New York City. They went door to door to be certain families had emotional and financial support. They discovered and met thousands of needs. They found children whose parents had gone to work that morning and never came home.

When God calls, we must be prepared to go. God will send us to other nations in person and/or through our pocket books. There are many language groups in the world that have no Bible and no Christian witness. We must be open to going to places few have been. Growing disciples will grow to the point that they will go out into the world. When God calls, be prepared to go.

Why must we be prepared to go? Jesus, just before He ascended to heaven, told His disciples, *"But you will receive power when the Holy Spirit comes on you; and you **will** be my witnesses in Jerusalem, and in all Judea and Samaria, and to the ends of the earth*"* (Acts 1:8, NIV). Notice that He said that we *will* go. We *will* go when we grow to the place in our lives where we know we have the Holy Spirit's power, and we go in that power.

*Jerusalem (your city); Judea (your state); Samaria (other parts of your nation); Ends of the earth (other nations and language groups).

Your Daily Walk

Scripture:
> Matthew 28:19-20

Application:
> Pray for another country today or person in another country that you may know.

Journal: _____

_____

_____

_____

_____

_____

_____

_____

_____

_____

_____

_____

_____

_____

_____

_____

_____

_____

_____

_____

Prayer: _____

_____

_____

_____

_____

_____

Grow and Multiply Yourself

"... and teach them to obey everything I have commanded you and I will be with you always, to the very end of the age" (Matthew 28:20, LPP).

Growing deep, wide and up is all about us. Growing out describes both missions and ministry, mainly to lost and hurting people. What do you do with new believers and immature believers? If you are not careful, you will fall into the trap of growing and reaching but not discipling. I was in that trap from the time I became a Christian (1970) until 1989. In 1989 I learned how to disciple others and now have a goal of seeing every new believer that we see come to Christ grow to the place that he/she learns to multiply himself/herself. This book is a product of the process that I have gone through and the goal that I have set for my life and ministry. There are four steps in the process of multiplying yourself. Jesus calls this "making disciples."

1. Reach (...make disciples...)

You will doubtlessly encounter people who believe in discipling, but think someone else should witness. Jesus never intended for the responsibilities of the Great Commission, Matthew 28:19-20, to be divided up and distributed to different groups.

The responsibility to witness, also known as evangelism, is not limited to Billy Graham, preachers, vocational evangelists and those who have the gift of evangelism. Every Christian is called to witness. Witnessing is the first step in making a disciple.

2. Baptize (...baptizing them...)

The next step is to teach your disciple to provide a witness to the world through baptism. In Week Three, baptism is explained as our first witness. Many churches are becoming open to the idea of allowing the one who witnesses to the new believer to baptize him/her. Even Paul, the model church planter in the New Testament, baptized only a handful of people (1 Corinthians 1:14-18). Who was baptizing? I presume the people of the church were baptizing.

Some churches allow new believers to choose who will baptize them. Sometimes the one who shared with the new believers baptizes them. Sometimes parents baptize children. We have seen older children baptize parents. Sometimes other pastors baptize, and sometimes the vocational ministers baptize.

I am not saying your church is wrong if only the pastor baptizes. However, some churches are discovering that more people are following the Great Commission because they have the freedom to reach and baptize those they reach.

3. Teach (...teaching them ...my commands...)

Many people believe that the essence of discipling is teaching. Teaching your disciple to study the Bible is important, but it is only one of four steps. Be sure to teach, but commit to reach and help new believers understand why it is important to follow Christ in believer's baptism. It is also important to note that Jesus wants us to begin our teaching by guiding disciples to read and learn what

He has said. Many people read parts of the Bible and form interpretations that do not properly reflect the life and words of Jesus. Learn what He said first and then shine the light of His words and ministry on everything else that you read and lead others to read and study. At **Itslifeministry.com**, you can get materials for a Bible study and in the near future the book I have written on the commands of Jesus. The title of the four quarters of Bible studies are *"What I Said"*.

4. Apply (...to obey...)

Jesus did not stop at the word *teach*. He said to teach disciples to obey or observe what He commanded. People can observe only what others are practicing. The final step is to learn, observe and then model and teach so that disciples can apply what they are being taught. Paul, in 1 Corinthians 13:1, said that if he knew everything, and was a dynamic speaker and a miracle worker, he would be nothing without applying love to his work. Multiplying yourself demands that you learn that a Christian does not learn just to have knowledge. We learn to grow. As we apply what we have learned, reach others for Jesus and teach them to obey Him, then we are multiplying our spiritual lives.

Your Daily Walk

Scripture:

1 Corinthians 13:1-13 (Read the entire chapter, but memorize verse 13.)

Memory verse: Remove the card that says "1 Corinthians 13:13" from your "To Learn" group and move it to your "Working to Memorize" group. Verse 13 is your second memory verse for this week and your twenty-second memory verse for this study.

Application:

Attempt to find a way to show God's love to someone today.

Journal: _____

_____

_____

_____

_____

_____

_____

_____

_____

_____

_____

_____

_____

Prayer: Ask God to help you be a person of love. _____

_____

_____

_____

A Time to Reflect, Recover and Review
Week 11, Day 7 - Saturday - Date: ____/____/_____

Slow down today and enhance your growth as a disciple. Review the week. Reflect on new material you have learned and insights you have underlined or highlighted. Return and read any material that you may have neglected to read and make journal entries on the days where you did not complete the assignments.

Let today be a day of spiritual recovery and reflection. Strive to meet with a discipler who can answer questions you may have and provide insights from what you have read. If you have done each day's assignment as designed, then enjoy this time of rest and review. Remember each day is important. Every study is designed to build on the foundation, Jesus, and construct the seven pillars of a Christian's faith: Prayer, Worship, Witness, Bible Study, Discipleship, Fellowship and Service.

Take time to be certain you have learned the two memory verses for this week and review the memory verses from the previous weeks.

Highlights from Week 11:
Read through each day of Week 11 and record a teaching from each day:
- Monday   - _____
_____
- Tuesday   - _____
_____
- Wednesday- _____
_____
- Thursday - _____
_____
- Friday   - _____
_____

Journal:
Take time to write in your journal. Write down ideas and record events that are impacting your life in Christ. Record the victories and the struggles, the concepts you are learning and those you still do not understand.

_____
_____
_____
_____
_____
_____

Prayer: Talk to God today. Listen to what He is saying to you.
Remember: Tomorrow is the traditional day to worship God. Whether your worship time is Friday night, Saturday or Sunday, ask God to help you to prepare before worship. Do not wait until your day of worship to rest and get ready. Prepare in advance so that you will get the most from worship.

Week 12

Build your Catch!

Most churches have business meetings. These can be confusing to new believers. You may encounter what a pastor friend of mine called "senator strong-throats". They love to hear themselves talk and want to believe they have some influence in the world. Unfortunately they often speak without much love and without much prayer. It often seems that they either want to start and argument or join an argument.

As I recalled many of the tense business meeting of years gone by, I realized that I could not remember a single "strong-throat" who was a soul-winner. Max Lucado says: "We (the Christians) are called to fish. When fishermen don't fish, they fight."[12] Max was right. These individuals, mostly men, were not consistently sharing their faith and they seemed to have plenty of time to fuss.

I have enjoyed being pastor of "fishing" churches. One was consistently in the top five among Alabama Baptist churches in baptisms. Another in the top ten and one in the top fifty. I led churches to limit their business meetings to three or four a year. The budgets of these churches were adopted in October, and the leadership was empowered to use and be good stewards of those resources. The finance committees were given the task of weekly watching the spending and keeping the church administrators accountable. These churches voted on only what they had to vote on; i.e. borrowing money, purchasing property or building facilities. Otherwise, they operated by consensus. The meetings began and ended with praise. What causes such a spirit of cooperation and trust? Lucado also says: "When churches fish, they flourish."[13]

Week 12 will help you learn why your church must fish to flourish. The third pillar of a Christian's walk is **Witness**. Week 12 helps you share your faith and guides you to tell others that Jesus lives in you. Being a positive living and verbal **witness** is essential to the multiplication of Christianity. Jesus calls witnesses "fishers," hence the title "Build your Catch!"

163

Be Committed to Worship
Week 12, Day 1 - Sunday - Date: _____/_____/_____

Sunday is a day of corporate worship. Most churches also offer small group Bible studies. Find time to honor God. Find a place where Christians are encouraged to worship, and the lost are invited to come to Christ.

Take your copy of *More Abundant LIFE* and take notes. The more you write, the more you will retain.

Worship includes giving and receiving. Pay attention to what you do in worship today. The Bible says, *"Therefore by Him let us continually **offer the sacrifice of praise** to God, that is, the fruit of our lips, giving thanks to His name."* (Hebrews 13:15, NKJ) Ask yourself these questions:

1. Did I give anything to God in worship today?   ___Yes ___No
2. Did I offer an acceptable sacrifice of praise?   ___Yes ___No
3. What did I receive from God? _____

The title of the pastor's message:_____
The main Bible text:_____
The main points of the pastor's message: _____
_____
_____
_____
_____
_____
_____
_____
_____
_____
_____

This is what I learned that I can apply to my life: _____
_____
_____
_____
_____

Prayer: "Lord, help me to apply your word to my life."
_____
_____
_____

Get a Rope!

"Though one may be overpowered by another, two can withstand him. And a threefold cord is not quickly broken" (Ecclesiastes 4:12, NKJ).

Being a witness for Christ is critically important. We must live for Christ, and we must tell others about Christ. Let me introduce you to the idea of spiritual warfare. Spiritual warfare comes in the form of attacks from an enemy who does not want us to apply the principles of the Bible to our lives. Jesus was attacked by Satan in the desert when Satan wanted to dethrone Him. He attacked Him by tempting His pride and hunger. Matthew 4:3 says, *"Now when the tempter came to Jesus, he said, 'If You are the Son of God, command that these stones become bread'"* (NKJ). Jesus did not come to the earth to be a walking magic show for the devil, nor did he need to prove anything to the devil. He simply quoted Deuteronomy 8:3, *"It is written, 'Man shall not live by bread alone, but by every word that proceeds from the mouth of God'"* (Matthew 4:4, NKJ).

Next, Satan tempted Him by attacking His knowledge of the word, and he wrongly used a passage from Psalm 91:11. *"If You are the Son of God, throw Yourself down. For it is written: 'He shall give His angels charge over you,' and, 'In their hands they shall bear you up, lest you dash your foot against a stone'"* (Matthew 4:6, NKJ). Again, Jesus resisted by quoting scripture correctly in Matthew 4:7. *"It is written again, 'You shall not tempt the LORD your God'"* (NIV; from Deuteronomy 6:6).

The third time Satan attacked Him and tempted Him with possessions. *"Again, the devil took Him up on an exceedingly high mountain, and showed Him all the kingdoms of the world and their glory. And he said to Him, 'All these things I will give You if You will fall down and worship me'"* (Matthew 4:8-9, NKJ). Jesus responded again by quoting scripture. *"Away with you, Satan! For it is written, 'You shall worship the LORD your God, and Him only you shall serve'"* (Matthew 4:10, NKJ, from Deuteronomy 6:13).

Jesus used scripture and prayed to overcome attacks. As you are applying the principles of the Bible, you will experience attempts from Satan to get you to turn away from your Christian walk, especially in the area of witnessing. The writer of Ecclesiastes gave us direction for overcoming these attacks. We form a band of three prayer partners. One, he says, may be overpowered, two can withstand, but when there are three of you, then you have a rope.

Have you noticed that ropes have three strands? I have often wondered if the first ropes were made by someone who read Ecclesiastes 4:12. I know that a single strand rope is a weak rope. Two strands give strength, but three strands give exponential strength.

Exodus 17 tells the story of Joshua taking the Israelites to battle. Moses stood on the hill. As long as the warriors could see Moses' hands in the air, they were winning. When his hands went down, they began to lose. Aaron, Moses' brother, and Hur came to the rescue. *"But Moses' hands were heavy; and they took a stone, and put it under him, and he sat thereon; and Aaron and Hur stayed up his hands, the one on the one side, and the other on the other side; and his hands were steady until the going down of the sun. So Joshua defeated Amalek and his people with the edge of the sword"* (Exodus 17:12-13, KJV). How many people were there on the hill? There were three. Moses was the leader and Aaron and Hur were his partners.

We must understand that God wants us to be witnesses. Those who read this book are likely doing so because someone witnessed to them. Let us be unselfish and share the good news of Jesus with others. We will find more help from God than we could have imagined. Witnesses will benefit from the three-strand rope of prayer to be powerful and effective witnesses.

Your Daily Walk

Scripture:
    Ecclesiastes 4:12

Memory verse: Remove the card that says "Ecclesiastes 4:12" from your "To Learn" group and move it to your "Working to Memorize" group. This is your first memory verse for week 12. It is your twenty-third for this study. When you get weary and need help, remember this verse and get two prayer partners.

Application:
    Pray with a prayer partner about learning to be a witness.

Journal: _____

_____

_____

_____

_____

_____

_____

_____

_____

_____

_____

_____

_____

_____

_____

_____

Prayer: _____

_____

_____

_____

_____

_____

Why Do I Need Shoes?
Week 12, Day 3 - Tuesday - Date: _____/_____/_____

"Wearing for shoes on your feet the eagerness to spread the gospel of peace" (Ephesians 6:15, NJB).

Week 5, Days 5 and 6 introduced you to the spiritual armor. You will recall that the third part of the spiritual armor is the shoes to spread the gospel of peace. As I look at the armor, I can understand two important truths.

1. There is protection that comes from witnessing. That seems to be a reversal from what I said yesterday, but it is not. You will need protection in order to prepare to witness, and you will receive protection from witnessing. That sentence is worth repeating. <u>You will need protection in order to prepare to witness, and you will receive protection from witnessing</u>. Think about it. Most of us are being told that when we witness, we will be attacked. I am convinced that the fear of attacks is why the reports show that about 95 percent of Christians have not witnessed and led another person to Christ. That is the attack! The attack comes when Satan tells us not to go. He does not want us to be protected. When we go, we are protected because we are being obedient to what Jesus called us to do. However, that protection is incomplete if we neglect the belt of truth, the breastplate of righteousness, the shield of faith, the helmet of salvation, the sword of the Spirit, and the connecting straps of prayer. Let's see how the enemy wants to steal our protection.

a. The belt of truth - The enemy wants us to live a lie and speak lies. God protects the livelihood of those who walk in truth.

b. The breastplate of righteousness - The enemy wants us to act in ways that are contrary to the Bible. He wants us to sin. God guides us to act with an attitude of doing what is right.

c. The shoes of preparation to share the gospel - The enemy knows we are saved, but does not want us to lead someone to Jesus. God protects those who are actively witnessing to become spiritual giants in their spiritual walk.

d. The shield of faith - The enemy wants us not to act unless we can see it or add it up. God protects Christians who walk by faith from Satan's external attacks. In fact He says that without faith we cannot please Him.

e. The helmet of salvation - The enemy wants us to feel like we live in a hopeless world and that we have no hope. God gives hope through Jesus. In 1 Thessalonians 5:8, Paul clarifies that the hope of our salvation is the helmet. That hope protects our minds from the tricks that the enemy tries to play on us.

f. The sword of the Spirit - The enemy does not want us to have a priority time that is spent studying the word of God. God protects and powerfully uses those who read, memorize, share and live by His word.

g. Prayer - The enemy does not want us to converse with God. God protects, connects and keeps in place every piece of the spiritual armor for those who both speak and listen to Him.

You need all seven parts to be complete. Therefore you need your shoes.

2.   The second truth about the shoes of witnessing came from a prayer. I asked God, "Why shoes?" Why is witnessing not the shield or sword or another part? In my priority time, God revealed to me that a soldier can go only so far without his shoes. I shared my revelation while preaching in Georgia. A woman approached me and explained that her husband was a POW in Vietnam. "The first thing they did when they captured him was to take off his boots", she replied.

Our enemy, the devil, has made most Christians his Prisoners of War. The world is a jungle of sinners needing the Savior. However, most will not put on the *"shoes of the preparation of the gospel of peace"* and go into the world. We need to remember that we can only go and grow so far without our shoes on.

Most Christians leave off this part of the spiritual armor. Jesus told us that His followers would fish. How is your catch? Are you willing to ask God to help you to put on the shoes of the preparation of the gospel of peace? Get ready to select two prayer partners. The next step comes tomorrow.

Your Daily Walk

Scripture:
Ephesians 6:15

Application:
Pray for God to help you walk in his protection.

Journal: _____

_____

_____

_____

_____

_____

_____

_____

_____

_____

_____

_____

_____

_____

_____

Prayer: _____

_____

_____

_____

_____

_____

Go Two by Two
Week 12, Day 4 - Wednesday - Date: _____/_____/_____

"And He called the twelve to Himself, and began to send them out two by two, and gave them power over unclean spirits" (Mark 6:7, NKJ).

The strength of witnessing is to go in pairs, not alone. Jesus was the discipler, and he sent the disciples in pairs. In a sense, there were three on the team, Jesus and the two disciples. The best method I have found for helping people to learn to put on the shoes of the gospel is for a discipler to take two disciples. During the first few weeks, the discipler demonstrates what the Bible has told us to do as we go. The disciples are, in the meantime, learning by watching, reading and memorizing scripture.

After a few weeks, the discipler begins to involve the disciples in the conversation. They begin by sharing their personal witness, which is something they know very well. At some point, they can share what the Bible says about becoming a Christian. Eventually, the disciples will be able to share the entire gospel plan and lead people to follow the Bible's plan for salvation. Finally, the disciples have grown to the place where they are now disciplers. It is time for them to pass on to two others what they have both seen and heard.

The first time I was introduced to the concept of teams of three was through Evangelism Explosion. In 1998 I became familiar with and involved in a ministry that was born from Evangelism Explosion called FAITH Sunday School/Evangelism Strategy. FAITH used teams of three, but attempted to build these teams from the same Sunday School class or age group. Most teams visited people who were in their age group.

In 2002 I was led to write a new witnessing ministry called *It's LIFE*. I wanted to teach more about involving new believers in small groups and to teach witnesses to follow up with those they were reaching. *It's LIFE* gave birth to *More Abundant LIFE*. If you are reading this book, you may have been reached because someone was discipled to witness to you through *It's LIFE*.

The concept of teams of three also helps to involve both men and women in the ministry. A team of two could not have a man and woman visiting together who are not husband and wife. A team of three could have two men and a woman or two women and a man. It provides a special level of accountability and protection against the enemy.

Learning to witness is going to be an important part of your spiritual growth. Ask a leader in your church to discover what ministry your church has that can disciple you to share your witness with non-Christians. If your church does not have a plan, then encourage your leaders to search for a way they can disciple the people of the church to tell others about Jesus. You can have them email me at lawrence.phipps@itslifeministry.com, and I will gladly talk to them about the ministry of *It's* LIFE that I developed while being of part of God building a church in Montgomery, Alabama from thirty-eight to over 2,500. You can also order a copy of the student version of *It's* LIFE at ItsLifeMinistry.com (click on bookstore). The book will have some blanks that only the Leader's Guide can complete, but the Appendices has the entire LIFE Gospel presentation.

Christians can become witnesses without being taught or led. They can become witnesses without a partner. They can become witnesses without a plan. Unfortunately, there are those who have been taught and led but do not witness as they should. There are those who had a partner and followed a plan, but have not continued to witness. However, most Christians who have never been discipled, had a partner and followed a plan will never witness. Tomorrow we will look at the plan.

Your Daily Walk

Scripture:
Mark 6:7

Application:
Do you know of someone who could disciple you to share your witness? Consider asking him/her if he/ she would.

Journal: _____

_____

_____

_____

_____

_____

_____

_____

_____

_____

_____

_____

_____

_____

_____

_____

_____

Prayer: _____

_____

_____

_____

_____

_____

_____

Find a Plan

Week 12, Day 5 - Thursday - Date: _____/_____/_____

"Then Philip opened his mouth, and beginning at this Scripture, preached Jesus to him" (Acts 8:35, NKJ).

Week 1, Day 3, outlines the gospel plan called LIFE. Why does it help a Christian to have a plan? As stated yesterday, few Christians will witness without the knowledge of how to organize and share the gospel. The first plan I wrote was in the early 1980's. It was called "Open the Door to Life." There were four points and four verses of scripture:

    1.   God has a plan for life. *"For God so loved the world that He gave His only begotten Son, that whoever believes in Him should not perish but have everlasting life"* (John 3:16, NKJ).

    2.   Man has a problem in life. *"For all have sinned, and come short of the glory of God"* (Romans 3:23, KJV).

    3.   God provides a solution to give life. *"God demonstrates His own love toward us, in that while we were yet sinners, Christ died for us"* (Romans 5:8, NKJ).

    4.   We must respond to receive life. *"If you confess with your mouth the Lord Jesus and believe in your heart that God has raised Him from the dead, you will be saved. For with the heart one believes unto righteousness, and with the mouth confession is made unto salvation"* (Romans 10:9 & 10, NKJ).

Notice something very important. There are more of God's words than mine. Salvation does not come because of our persuasive speech, but by the drawing of God's Holy Spirit. His Holy Spirit works when we share the words from the Bible.

In the space below I compare what Peter shared in Acts 2 to the LIFE outline of the gospel presentation. He was talking to Jews on the first Christian Pentecost and explained to them how to have LIFE.

Acts 2:22: *"Men of Israel, hear these words; Jesus of Nazareth, a man approved of God among you by miracles and wonders and signs, which God did by Him in the midst of you, as you yourselves also know...*- God **L**oves people!

    23 *"Him, being delivered by the determinate counsel and foreknowledge of God, you have taken, and by wicked hands have crucified and slain...*- People are **I**mperfect.

    24 *"Whom God has raised up, having loosed the pains of death: because it was not possible that death should keep its hold on Him. 32 This Jesus has God raised up, whereof we all are witnesses. 36 Therefore let all the house of Israel know assuredly, that God has made that same Jesus, whom ye have crucified, both Lord and Christ. 37 Now when they heard this, they were pricked in their heart, and said unto Peter and to the rest of the apostles, Men and brethren, what shall we do? 38 Then Peter said unto them, Repent, and be baptized every one of you in the name of Jesus Christ for the forgiveness of sins...*- God offers **F**orgiveness.

    38b *"And you shall receive the gift of the Holy Spirit. 41 Then they that gladly received his word were baptized: and the same day there were added unto them*

171

about three thousand souls." - We can have **E**ternal life.

Note: The book of Acts describes the launching of the New Testament church. In the twenty-eight chapters of Acts Luke records that the gospel is shared seventeen times and is talked about another eighteen times. If the sharing of the gospel and people being saved consumed the Apostles as they launched the church, we must believe that God intends for it to consume the believers and the churches of the twenty-first century.

There are times when I share what Peter said, or something similar, with an unbeliever, and God's Spirit works through His word and Spirit, and causes the person to whom I am talking to want to be a Christian. When this happens, I lead him or her to pray and tell God what he or she wants. People will learn various packages to memorize and share the gospel until Jesus returns, but it is still the words from the Bible that make the difference. We can develop various memory tools, but God's word is still salvation's tool. Find a plan, learn scripture, and love sharing.

(Materials for learning and teaching the LIFE evangelism/discipleship process may be obtained at the Bookstore of ItsLifeMinistry.com.)

Your Daily Walk

Scripture:

Romans 10:9-10

Memory verses: Remove the card that says "Romans 10:9-10" from your "To Learn" group and move it to your "Working to Memorize" group. Romans 10:9-10 are your next memory verses for *More Abundant LIFE*. They may be some of the most important you will memorize. The guide to eternal life is contained within these two verses. Work to memorize them.

Application:

Prepare to enroll in a ministry to be discipled to be a witness.

Journal: _____

_____

_____

_____

_____

_____

_____

_____

_____

_____

_____

Prayer: _____

_____

_____

_____

_____

Follow Jesus' Command
Week 12, Day 6 - Friday - Date: _____/_____/_____

The first command that Jesus gave His followers is recorded in Matthew 4:19, *"Then He said to them, 'Follow Me, and I will make you fishers of men'"* (NKJ). The Bible says, *"They immediately left their nets and followed Him"* (Matthew 4:20). The last command of Jesus was, *"But you shall receive power when the Holy Spirit has come upon you; and you shall be witnesses to Me in Jerusalem, and in all Judea and Samaria, and to the end of the earth"* (Acts 1:8, NKJ). This week *was* entitled "Build your catch." Jesus called the Christians to be fishers of men. We are to catch souls for the Kingdom.

Jesus did not give the above commands and make His lifestyle about winning the lost because He wanted us to do everything but win people to Him. You became a Christian because someone cared enough to share with you the truth of eternal life. You are reading this book because someone cared enough to help you grow as a disciple. Now you have the responsibility of preparing yourself to make disciples.

Imagine that the closest person to you had what was thought to be an incurable disease. However, a new treatment was found that would give your friend a long life. How would you feel if no one shared the treatment with your friend, and you had to watch him/her die?

There are over five billion people in the world who are sick in their trespasses and sins. We have the cure; His name is Jesus. How do you think these people will feel a thousand years from now if we refuse to tell them how to be saved and refuse to give them an opportunity to receive eternal life? Have we as Christians become so cruel and selfish that we are glad we have been cured, but we will not share it with others?

Be aware that those who die without Christ will be in a Christless eternity 1,000 years from now. I heard the late Dr. R. G. Lee preach at an evangelism conference in Alabama in 1972 when I was a high school senior. Dr. Lee said, "If hell were a place where people go and get out in ten years, I would never preach on hell. If hell were a place where people go and get out in a hundred years, I would never preach on hell. If hell were a place where people go and get out in a thousand years, I would never preach on hell. But hell is a place where those without Christ go, and they never get out."

As growing disciples, we need to recognize that hell is a real place. We talk about being saved. We are saved from hell and saved to an eternity in heaven. Hell is a place for those who die without Christ. Jesus said the road there is wide, and many are finding it. The road to heaven is narrow, and few are finding it. Why is the road so narrow? The answer is painfully simple. Too few Christians are sharing with their family, friends, co-workers and neighbors about how to get to heaven.

The command is clear. Jesus said that followers will become fishers. If you and I are not fishing, then we are not following what Jesus commanded us to do. These may be strong words. They often offend people who do not want to be convicted about their poor or nonexistent Christian witness. Some will criticize you. Their goal will be to bring you down because they do not want to rise to the challenge to prepare to be a living, verbal witness. Do not take the bait. Keep witnessing and allow God to convict them until they become witnesses.

To be a fisher of men, you will need a rope, your shoes, a partner, a plan and a command. This week you have received each of these. Now it is time to go and make disciples!!!

Your Daily Walk

Scripture:
Matthew 4:19

Application:
Ask God to help you become a fisher of souls.

Journal: _____

_____
_____
_____
_____
_____
_____
_____
_____
_____
_____
_____
_____
_____
_____
_____
_____
_____
_____

Prayer: _____

_____
_____
_____
_____
_____
_____
_____

A Time to Reflect, Recover, and Review
Week 12, Day 7 - Saturday - Date: ____/____/_____

Week 12 is designed to encourage the reader to learn to share his/her faith and disciple others to do so. Let me recommend that you read through the chapter again. You will gain more insights than you did the first time you went through the week. Read your journal entries and make notes about answered prayers and spiritual growth.

Let today be a day of spiritual recovery and reflection. Strive to meet with a discipler who can answer questions you may have and provide insights from what you have read. If you have done each day's assignment as designed, then enjoy this time of rest and review. Remember each day is important. Every study is designed to build on the foundation, Jesus, and construct the seven pillars of a Christian's faith: Prayer, Worship, Witness, Bible Study, Discipleship, Fellowship and Service.

Take time to be certain you have learned the two memory verses for this week and review the memory verses from the entire book.

Highlights from Week 12:
Read through each day of Week 2 and record a teaching from each day:
- Monday   - _____

_____
- Tuesday   - _____

_____
- Wednesday-_____

_____
- Thursday - _____

_____
- Friday   - _____

_____

Journal:
Take time to write in your journal. Write down ideas and record events that are impacting your life in Christ. Record the victories and the struggles, the concepts you are learning and those you still do not understand.

_____

_____

_____

_____

_____

Prayer: Talk to God today. Listen to what He is saying to you.

Remember: Tomorrow is the traditional day to worship God. Whether your worship time is Friday night, Saturday or Sunday, ask God to help you to prepare before worship. Do not wait until your day of worship to rest and get ready. Prepare in advance so that you will get the most from worship.

Week 13

Build God's Community

The book *Growing Sunday School/Small Group TEAMS* (available at the ItsLifeMinistry.com bookstore) designs classes to take care of people. The "**M**" in TEAMS is the Ministry Coordinator (MC). The MC enlists Care Group Leaders and a Fellowship Coordinator who help classes love and minister to people. Do not be deceived into believing that you can only have good fellowship if you keep the class together and of "manageable size." Hear this Biblical parable for the 21st century:

The group was small. There were only eleven men and a few women. After a lot of prayer and tossing the dice, another man was let into the group. They sat in their upper floor Sunday School classroom, prayed and sought for something to happen. It did. God's Spirit came into the room. He divided the class, called many to preach and the city experienced the greatest world-impacting one day revival anyone would ever see.

How did this small group lead the infusion of thousands of people? They did not do it by staying in their classroom. There is no evidence they ever returned to their upper room. They did not get stuck admiring their new teachers so much that they could not hear the Father say "go." You do not handle the masses by sitting when you should be serving, getting when you should be giving, and gathering when you should be going.

Aren't you glad that when the Holy Spirit "divided" that small class in Acts 2 that they gladly spoke, shared, welcomed, went and even died for church growth? I am, because I am a product of their unselfish "Upper Room" Sunday School class. So are you!   -LP

The sixth pillar of a Christian's life is **Fellowship**. The goal of Week 13 is to guide the believer to understand how God expands fellowship to build His church. Week 13 focuses the reader on the community of faith, the church. Pray for God to help you learn how to build up the church which is "the bride of Christ."

Be Committed to Worship

Week 13, Day 1 - Sunday - Date: _____/_____/_____

Sunday is a day of corporate worship. Most churches also offer small group Bible studies. Find time to honor God. Find a place where Christians are encouraged to worship, and the lost are invited to come to Christ.

Take your copy of *More Abundant LIFE* and take notes. The more you write, the more you will retain.

Worship includes giving and receiving. Pay attention to what you do in worship today. The Bible says, *"Therefore by Him let us continually **offer the sacrifice of praise** to God, that is, the fruit of our lips, giving thanks to His name."* (Hebrews 13:15, NKJ) Ask yourself these questions:

1. Did I give anything to God in worship today?   ___Yes ___No
2. Did I offer an acceptable sacrifice of praise?   ___Yes ___No
3. What did I receive from God? _____

The title of the pastor's message:_____
The main Bible text:_____
The main points of the pastor's message: _____

_____
_____
_____
_____
_____
_____
_____
_____
_____
_____

This is what I learned that I can apply to my life: _____

_____
_____
_____

Prayer: "Lord, help me to apply your word to my life."

_____
_____
_____
_____

How can I Love the Church? - Part 1
Week 13, Day 2 - Monday - Date: _____/_____/_____

"One of them, an expert in the law, tested Him with this question: "Teacher, which is the greatest commandment in the Law?" Jesus replied: "'Love the Lord your God with all your heart and with all your soul and with all your mind.' This is the first and greatest commandment. And the second is like it: 'Love your neighbor as yourself.' All the Law and the Prophets hang on these two commandments" (Matthew 22:35-40, NIV).

One of the religious leaders was testing Jesus. "Which is the greatest commandment?" He asked. He no doubt was thinking of the Ten Commandments or the Jewish law. Jesus returned to the Jewish law in Deuteronomy 6:5. Memorizing scripture helped Him know the answer. He told the man that the greatest commandment is to love God. Next, He expanded His words and told them that the second commandment is to love people.

You are getting near the end of the Sunday School edition of *More Abundant LIFE*. The message of fellowship is central to growing a class or expanding a small group. When people come to Bible study, they hear teachings on the word of God. However, many come because of the fellowship that is offered. Remember, the number one response people give to attending a small group or worship service is "a friend." People are looking for friends who genuinely love them. The last three decades in our society have taught most people to spot the phonies. In the 1970's there was a musical with a song that had the words, "Don't be a phony, because a phony never wins."

Several years ago, I sat in a community meeting and listened to a gentleman pray a beautiful prayer. His words were well chosen, his knowledge and admiration of God seemed sincere. Later I learned that out of anger he had not spoken to his sister in years. He often walked out of his church's worship service because he did not like a staff member, and he caused a woman to cry when he made a racial remark about some orphaned children she brought to his church. He appeared like a phony to everyone who knew him.

We cannot love God when we will not love people. The words of 1 John 4:20-21 are convicting. *"If anyone says, "I love God," yet hates his brother, he is a liar. For anyone who does not love his brother, whom he has seen, cannot love God, whom he has not seen. And he has given us this command: Whoever loves God must also love his brother"* (NIV). A growing disciple will learn the importance of loving people. The more you grow, the more you will learn to love God by loving people. You will learn to love people by sharing a smile, an encouraging word and a good deed.

Paul goes one more step. He tells Christians that while we are to do good to everyone, we should pay close attention to doing good to other believers (Galatians 6:10). Be careful to understand that your brothers and sisters in Christ are not the enemy. God wants His children to get along so that the rest of the world will want to join God's family. Would you want to be adopted by a family whose members hate each other? No one would. The Christian community can be God's best promotion or greatest obstruction.

Love in the church begins with a personal desire to love. As you grow as a believer, you will learn how important it is to have unconditional love. People are imperfect. They will disappoint and hurt you. When we return hatred for hurt, it changes us for the worse, and those who hurt us hardly notice, if at all. When we return love to those who hurt us or others in the church, it builds us up and irritates them. *"If your enemy is hungry, feed him; if he is thirsty, give him something to drink. In doing this, you will heap burning coals on his head. Do not be overcome by evil, but overcome evil with good"* (Romans 12:20-21, NIV).

When there is love in your Christian life, it is an overflow of God's Spirit working in you. On our own, we can like people and help people. The concept of biblical love is not man-made; it is God-given. The man described in the earlier story had a religion, including a church, but he lacked a growing relationship. A growing relationship will produce love that builds up the body of Christ. Love His church enough to grow in Him.

Your Daily Walk

Scripture:

1 John 4:20-21

Application:

Learn to maintain love in the church.

Journal: _____

_____

_____

_____

_____

_____

_____

_____

_____

_____

_____

_____

_____

_____

Prayer: _____

_____

_____

_____

_____

_____

How can I Love the Church? - Part 2

Christ loved the church and gave Himself up for her" (Ephesians 5:25, NIV).

The Bible teaches believers that Jesus died for the church and for those who are not saved. If Jesus thought the church was important enough for Him to die for, we must believe the church is important enough for us to live and work within it. Yesterday we said that loving the church begins with love coming from the believer. Today I want to explain how important it is to God that we love His church.

God led me to begin a church in 1994. During my first seventeen years as a pastor, I had been called to be pastor of four different churches. Several of these churches had been damaged by dissension in the past and had a difficult time reestablishing themselves as vibrant churches in the present. When we began Vaughn Forest Church in Montgomery, Alabama, we began with a members' covenant. One part of the covenant said that members would speak positively about the church. We explained that we were not just talking about our church; we were talking about every church of the Lord, Jesus Christ. Ephesians 5 presents the analogy of the church being the bride of Christ. Jesus is often referred to as the Bridegroom. He is a faithful Bridegroom. What faithful, loving husband would want someone to criticize his bride? I can tell you that husbands who love their wives would not stand for someone else's criticizing and belittling them.

Do we believe that Jesus is any different? Would He want someone criticizing His bride, the church? You and I both know that those who criticize the bride of Jesus will be guilty before God. Will a covenant to speak positively about the church keep unspiritual people from speaking negatively about the bride of Christ? It will not. However, recognizing how Jesus wants us, the Christians, to be a precious part of a marvelous body and to lift up the entire bride of Christ helps people to recognize when they are moving away from the will of God.

How can you and I as believers be positive influences in the church? First we can correct any conflicts that we may have among other Christians. Several years ago, I visited a family who had shown interest in becoming a part of our church. During the conversation the husband constantly criticized his previous church. After several minutes, I interrupted and explained: "There may come a time when God wants you to be a part of our church. However, He will never lead you to us until you correct these broken relationships." It would have been a mistake for me to welcome him to our church with the negative baggage he was carrying.

Many Christians try to cure their conflicts by running from the church. Those who join a church because they are running from a conflict will, in a few short years, run from the new church for similar reasons. As a believer, please do not emulate the actions of Christians who have been taught some negative lessons instead of loving and living in the church.

A second way to be a positive influence is to gently correct others who are criticizing the bride of Christ. Paul tells us, *"No longer be children, but learn to speak the truth in love and grow up in Christ who causes growth of the body for the edifying of itself in love"* (Ephesians 4:14-16, LPP). As a believer, you have both the right and responsibility to gently correct those of us who are wrong. I recall a new believer asking an older believer about tithing. The older believer, who was obviously not one who tithed, tried to dissuade the new believer from tithing. "Does the Bible teach giving?" asked the new believer. "Well, yes," replied the older believer. "Then if it is okay with you, I believe I will give." The new believer did not directly tell the other believer that he was wrong, but he indirectly corrected him by letting him know that he was interested in doing what the Bible says.

The third and most important way to positively influence the fellowship of the church is to pray for the church. I have discovered that the more I pray for people, the less I am prone to criticize them. Pray for your church by praying for the members by name. Satan wants to tear down the body of Christ. Through prayer let us build up the fellowship.

Your Daily Walk

Scripture:

Matthew 22:37 records Jesus quoting from Deuteronomy 6:5.

Memory verse: Remove the card that says "Deuteronomy 6:5" from your "To Learn" group and move it to your "Working to Memorize" group. You will notice that you have already memorized this from Matthew 22.

Application:

Learn to be a positive influence.

Journal: _____

_____
_____
_____
_____
_____
_____
_____
_____
_____
_____

Prayer: _____

_____
_____
_____
_____
_____

I Want to Be Sharp!

"Iron is sharpened by iron, one person is sharpened by contact with another." (Proverbs 27:17, NJB)

Fellowship in the church is more than getting together for times of meeting and eating. The church is the congregation of Christians. I once believed that I was the church. I am not the church, but I am a part of the church if I am gathering with other believers. The word "church" comes from a Greek word *ekklesia* which translates "the called out." There are those who want to be loners. They seek to be spiritual hermits. They often claim that they can worship by themselves on the lake, in the mountains or at the beach. They can worship by themselves, but they cannot be the church by themselves. Let us not become solitary Christians. Let's be a part of the bride of Christ. Let us love the bride, encourage the bride, learn from the bride and grow as a part of the bride. I have often exclaimed that if as many people are worshiping on the lake and at the beach as say they are, then we need to get there in a hurry because revival is about to break out as has rarely been seen. To be fair, I have enjoyed times of worship at the lake, in the mountains and at the beach. However, my regular time of worship is with the church. My strength comes from the Lord, but it often comes through the church.

A great benefit of the church comes from Christians sharpening one another. My greatest accountability partner is Jesus. There are people to whom I am accountable, also. I often meet with them, pray with them and exchange insights from the Bible with these individuals. I become spiritually sharper because of them, and my goal is for them to become spiritually sharper because of me. The importance of fellowship in the body cannot be overemphasized. Take time to commit to the body of Christ so that you can gain from the body of Christ.

Hebrews 10:24 says that we should find ways to encourage each other and to challenge each other to produce good deeds. The most effective method I have found for sharpening someone else and spurring him/her to positively produce is to model what I am teaching.

How does iron sharpen iron? Notice that one piece of iron cannot sharpen another piece of iron by simply placing the two close to each other. Fellowship involves Christians learning to be close to each other, but it also involves work. The pieces of iron must work together in order to sharpen each other.

Understand that the sharpening process always produces friction. As a young pastor, I would often be concerned when I would pray, implement a plan, people would be saved, and invariably, a small group would begin to complain about something. A wonderful Christian woman once told me, "Bro. Lawrence, remember that forward motion always produces friction." The beautiful part of the work of the church and the interaction of Christians is not the absence of friction, but the presence of Christ who takes interpersonal conflicts, teaches us how to overcome them and makes us into stronger Christians, and His church becomes a strong body.

You may be meeting with someone who is sharpening you right now. If you are, then thank God. Most Christians never had someone to sharpen them. If you do not have someone, then begin to pray. If you are a man, then look for another man to whom you can be accountable and who will encourage and sharpen you. If you are a woman, then look for another woman. It is never a good idea for a man and woman who are not husband and wife to meet together to try to build each other spiritually. Protect yourself from a trap of the enemy and find someone who is your gender with whom you can meet. By the way, this rule also applies to unmarried students. I know of very few examples where a male and female student came together to sharpen each other, and spiritual growth followed.

Your Daily Walk

Scripture:
Proverbs 27:17

Application:
Who is sharpening you? _____
Who are you sharpening? _____

Journal: _____

_____
_____
_____
_____
_____
_____
_____
_____
_____
_____
_____
_____
_____
_____
_____
_____

Prayer: _____

_____
_____
_____
_____
_____
_____

What if They Won't Agree with Me?

Being in fellowship with the body of Christ should not rest on total agreement from everyone. Interpretations about the meaning and practice of scripture are wide and varied. According to 1 Corinthians 1:10, God's intent is that believers search God's will and seek understanding that ultimately brings agreement. God's goal, however, is that disciples learn to love.

Jesus, in John 13:34-35 said, *"A new commandment I give to you, that you love one another; as I have loved you, that you also love one another. By this all will know that you are My disciples, if you have love for one another"* (NKJ). Notice three important insights that Jesus gave through these verses.

1.   Love is a command, not a suggestion. Jesus preached and practiced unconditional love. This is not an option for the Christian; it is absolutely essential to growing in Christ. When we love people in the body who do not agree with us, then we receive love from individuals in the body during those times when we discover that we are the ones who were wrong.

2.   We are to love the way that Jesus loves us. Galatians 6:7 says, *"Do not be deceived: God cannot be mocked. A man reaps what he sows."* God created this universe on the principle of sowing and reaping. When a farmer plants corn, he gets corn not cotton. When a farmer plants tomatoes, he gets tomatoes not turnips. Whatever he puts in the ground is what comes up. The same is true of Christians. When believers love others, then they receive love. When we encourage, we are encouraged. When we love, we are loved. Conversely, when we discourage, we are discouraged. When we will not forgive, we are not forgiven. Everyday you and I are planting our crop. Plant a crop that you will enjoy harvesting.

Paul says that we reap what we sow. The principles of sowing and reaping also tell me that we reap because we sow, we reap later than we sow, and we reap more than we sow. Make it your goal as a growing Christian to be planting a crop that you will enjoy harvesting.

3.   Love is a command; it is to be sown because Jesus loves us, and it testifies to our discipleship or lack of it. *"By this* (by loving one another) *all will know that you are my disciples"* (John 13:35, LPP). If someone looks at your attitude toward people and the church today, what would they see? Would they see love or hatred? Would they see cooperation or confusion? Would they see a growing disciple or an uncertain hypocrite?

People, especially those who are without Christ, are watching us. They want to know if we are real, righteous and whether our life is worth following. A professional athlete, when confronted about his poor example explained that he was not a role model and never intended to be. Christians do not have this luxury. We are God's advertisement of those who love the fellowship, or else we are a negative example of those who hurt the fellowship. Regardless of whether or not we always agree, we are still commanded to love.

As you grow as a believer, you will learn that the church is under constant attack. Satan is doing everything he can to tear down the church. The enemy will use each of us to help him if we are not careful. Keep your eyes on Jesus. Be diligent to love and care for those in the body. Seek agreement, but understand that there will be times of disagreement. Disagreements do not mean that the others are all wrong or that you are totally correct. Pray for those with whom you disagree to discover how to live at peace within the body of Christ.

Your Daily Walk

Scripture:

John 13:34-35

Memory verses: Remove the card that says "John 13:34-35" from your "To Learn" group and move it to your "Working to Memorize" group. John 13:34-35 is your second memory passage for this week.

Application:

Become a consistent disciple.

Journal: _____

_____

_____

_____

_____

_____

_____

_____

_____

_____

_____

_____

_____

_____

_____

_____

_____

_____

_____

Prayer: _____

_____

_____

_____

_____

_____

_____

Can trials build fellowship?

Week 13, Day 6 - Friday - Date: ____/____/_____

You have already learned that life in Christ is not trouble free. Your work to build fellowship in the church will often best be seen when others are hurting. In 1990 I visited a home and ministered to a family who had stopped attending church eight years earlier. I reenrolled them in Sunday School. Class members followed up with them, they began attending again and made new commitments of their lives to Christ. About a year later, the wife became ill and died. During that time, the fellowship of believers, including the ministers, visited, called, prayed, brought food and generally encouraged the family. In a few weeks, a paid ad appeared in the local paper. It was a note to the community thanking the church for their ministry.

You will discover Christians who have disconnected from the fellowship of the church. You should care enough to help them reconnect to the church. In the body of believers, Christians will discover the love of believers, ministry in times of need and encouragement when they need it most. As a Christian you should not just wait for others to reach out to you. You should reach out to others.

Fellowship is built from within as we grow as disciples and learn to love. Fellowship is built from attitudes that are formed to love the church and the people who make up the church. Fellowship is built when our love is not contingent on people thinking just like us and fellowship is built through ministry.

Here are some helpful guidelines for ministering within the body.

1.   Minister through prayer. Of all the things you can do, prayer will be the most important. James 5:16 instructs us to pray for each other. When we pray we are involving God in the lives of the people we love. We can reach out to ask God to help them and at the same time discover that a willingness to pray helps us. The fellowship of ministry often begins with followers praying.

2.   Minister purposefully. Ephesians 5:16 tells us to make the most of every opportunity. Look for ministry opportunities instead of waiting until someone calls. After comedian Grady Nutt died, his wife, Eleanor, came to speak to a seminar I was attending. She explained that the words which meant the least to her were, "If there is anything I can do, let me know." The words that were most meaningful were those that offered specific requests. "Eleanor, would you allow me to bring supper on Friday?" However, the most meaningful were the ones who were like her neighbor who noticed her dog was digging a hole under the fence. He simply took his shovel and filled in the hole. There are times we need to ask, and there are times we simply need to act.

3.   Minister without thought of reward. Jesus told us in Matthew 6:1-4 not to minister in order to be recognized. If we help people so that we will be applauded, then the applause is our reward. There are times when we will be applauded. There is nothing wrong with recognition. The problem comes when we seek recognition. Jesus told us to let our lights shine so that people see our good works, and we can give God the glory. Ministry will be one of the greatest

ways your light will shine. When the tough times come, you can minister to those who are going through trials. Your work in other believers' lives will build the fellowship and will glorify God. Remember a great deal could be accomplished in the church if nobody cared who got the credit. Better still an enormous amount could be done in and through the church if all the believers made certain that God received the credit. The fellowship of believers needs people who are selfless, God-glorifying Christians.

When is the last time you helped someone anonymously. A great joy comes to us when we give something that costs us to someone who cannot repay us and know that only God knows what we did. Take time to practice anonymous love today. What you do in secret, God will see and be pleased.

Your Daily Walk

Scripture:
    Matthew 6:1-4
Application:
    Learn to minister to others without thought of reward.
Journal: _____

_____
_____
_____
_____
_____
_____
_____
_____
_____
_____
_____
_____
_____
_____
_____
_____
_____
_____

Prayer: _____

_____
_____
_____
_____
_____
_____
_____

A Time to Reflect, Recover and Review
Week 13, Day 7 - Saturday - Date: _____/_____/_____

Reviewing and reflecting allows us to enhance our growth as disciples. Review the week. Reflect on new material you have learned and insights you have underlined or highlighted. Return and read any material that you may have neglected to read and make journal entries on the days where you did not complete the assignments.

Let today be a day of spiritual recovery and reflection. Strive to meet with a discipler who can answer questions you may have and provide insights from what you have read. If you have done each day's assignment as designed, then enjoy this time of rest and review. Remember each day is important. Every study is designed to build on the foundation, Jesus, and construct the seven pillars of a Christian's faith: Prayer, Worship, Witness, Bible Study, Discipleship, Fellowship and Service.

Take time to be certain you have learned the two memory verses for this week and review the memory verses from the previous weeks.

Highlights from Week 13:
Read through each day of Week 13 and record a teaching from each day:
- Monday - _____

- Tuesday - _____

- Wednesday- _____

- Thursday - _____

- Friday   - _____

Journal:
Take time to write in your journal. Write down ideas and record events that are impacting your life in Christ. Record the victories and the struggles, the concepts you are learning and those you still do not understand.

_____
_____
_____
_____
_____
_____

Prayer: Talk to God today. Listen to what He is saying to you.

Remember: Tomorrow is the traditional day to worship God. Whether your worship time is Friday night, Saturday or Sunday, ask God to help you to prepare before worship. Do not wait until your day of worship to rest and get ready. Prepare in advance so that you will get the most from worship.

Week 14

Build your Contribution

It was the custom in Jesus' day for the least of all the servants in the house to meet guests at the door, remove their shoes and wash their feet. The night that Jesus was betrayed, He arose from the meal, got a basin of water and a towel and began to wash His disciples' feet. He knew that one disciple would leave within minutes to get His accusers and bring them to arrest Him. He had already prophesied that another, Peter, would, in a few hours, stand defiantly in the courtyard and swear that he did not know Jesus. Nine of the men who feared that the cross would be their fate, would scatter. One would stand at the foot of the cross with the women as Jesus gave instructions for caring for His family.

Why would Jesus wash twenty-four dirty, defiant feet of men who would soon disappoint Him? Matthew holds the answer when he records Jesus saying that the Son of Man did not come to be served but to serve and to give His life as a ransom for many (20:28). He came to serve those who would betray Him, deny Him, leave Him and criticize Him. He did not serve to receive applause, and He didn't quit when He wasn't appreciated. People did not pay Him, give Him a plague, prize or position. He was a perfect servant and He was given a cross.

Why do you serve, or why did you quit? Jesus finished washing the disciples' feet and then told them, and us, that He did this so that they, and we, would serve others in the same way He served them, and us. We do not serve for what we will get, but because of what we have been given, eternal life.

The seventh pillar of a Christian's life is **Service**. Jesus left us here to serve. Week 14 will guide the reader through the five important steps to serve. Each of the five days will follow the acrostic **SERVE** to help you remember the component parts of applying what you are learning about yourself for the glory of God and edification of His church. Prepare to build your contribution.

Be Committed to Worship
Week 14, Day 1 - Sunday - Date: _____/_____/_____

Sunday is a day of corporate worship. Most churches also offer small group Bible studies. Find time to honor God. Find a place where Christians are encouraged to worship, and the lost are invited to come to Christ.

Take your copy of *More Abundant LIFE* and take notes. The more you write, the more you will retain.

Worship includes giving and receiving. Pay attention to what you do in worship today. The Bible says, *"Therefore by Him let us continually **offer the sacrifice of praise** to God, that is, the fruit of our lips, giving thanks to His name."* (Hebrews 13:15, NKJ) Ask yourself these questions:

1. Did I give anything to God in worship today?   ___Yes ___No
2. Did I offer an acceptable sacrifice of praise?   ___Yes ___No
3. What did I receive from God? _____

The title of the pastor's message:_____
The main Bible text:_____
The main points of the pastor's message: _____

_____
_____
_____
_____
_____
_____
_____
_____
_____
_____
_____
_____

This is what I learned that I can apply to my life:

_____
_____
_____

Prayer: "Lord, help me to apply your word to my life."

_____
_____
_____

SERVE - Part 1

Spiritual Gifts - The first step to SERVE
Week 14, Day 2 - Monday - Date: _____/_____/_____

"*Each one should use whatever gift he has received to* **serve** *others, faithfully administering God's grace in its various forms*" (1 Peter 4:10, NIV).

Every believer has spiritual gifts. Last week we discussed love which the Bible calls the "most excellent" gift (1 Corinthians 12:31; 13:13). Today we will introduce the believer to other gifts.

The first part of *More Abundant LIFE* discusses how God uses spiritual gifts in the believer to benefit both the body of Christ and the world (1 Corinthians 12:7). Most people have two or three strong gifts that define who they are in Christ. A spiritual gift can be defined as the way that the Holy Spirit who lives in you wants to work through your life. One way that God's Spirit works through me is preaching. Preaching is not the only gift I have, but it defines me more than any other gift. God has also provided me with the gifts of evangelism, administration and giving. The Holy Spirit works through me to motivate others to witness, administrate the work of His church and contribute to the ministry of the church.

God wants your life to be characterized by meaningful service. He has supernaturally endowed you for the task. When you serve according to your gifts, you will grow stronger and your contribution will be more powerful. On the other hand, if you ignore your gifts and try to serve outside of your God-given expertise, you will grow slowly and contribute less.

Years ago I administered a spiritual gifts inventory to a church group. At one of the breaks a man approached me with a very unhappy tone and exclaimed, "I hate these tests. Every time I take one, it says my gift is *helps*." I knew the man. I was not surprised that God had given him the gifts of helps. God wanted to develop the man's servant heart, but he wanted to be "in charge" of something. God could not give him more responsibility until he was faithful with what he had been given. When you discover your gifts and faithfully use them, God will increase what you have and what you can do.

The goal of spiritual gifts is to glorify God, build up the body and bring the world to Jesus. Read 1 Corinthians 12:12-31. Paul makes an analogy between the physical body and the body of Christ. He points out that every part is important. When one part hurts, we all hurt; we cannot all be the same part.

Have you ever bumped your little toe into a chair leg or bed post? That toe is small and seems insignificant until it is hit, then the whole body aches. The body could survive without the toe, but not as well. Additionally, we would have a problem if we had ten little toes on our feet and ten on our hands. Begin to search for your gifts. You are important to God, to the church and the world.

Try to find a spiritual gifts survey that will help you locate how God's Spirit wants to work through you.

There is a simple inventory provided in the book *Growing Sunday School/ Small Group TEAMS* that is designed specifically for small groups or Sunday School classes (*Growing Sunday School TEAMS* is available at ItsLifeMinistry.com).

There are more extensive spiritual inventories, such as the one available through WillowCreek Community Church called *NetWork*. However, the *"TEAMS"* survey is a great place for a person to begin to investigate how to get involved according to his/her spiritual gifts. By the way, the inventory available in the *"TEAMS"* book gives a church permission to reproduce for use within Sunday School classes or small groups. Below is a list of some places of service within the Sunday School that are listed in TEAMS. See if one or more of these gifts identifies you or interests you:

Teacher, Evangelism leader, Administrator, Mininistry Coordinator or Care Group Leader, Service Coordinator, Fellowship Coordinator, Prayer Leader, among others.

Sunday School is the largest organism in most churches. It is also the largest entry point. The Sunday School class is a great place to help people begin to use their spiritual gifts and get involved in service.

Your Daily Walk

Scripture:

1 Corinthians 12:1-11

Application:

Name a gift you believe you have. _____

Journal: _____

_____

_____

_____

_____

_____

_____

_____

_____

_____

_____

_____

_____

Prayer: _____

_____

_____

_____

_____

SERVE

Experience - The second step to SERVE
Week 14, Day 3 - Tuesday - Date: ____/____/_____

"Delight yourself in the LORD and he will give you the desires of your heart" (Psalm 37:4, NIV). When we discover our spiritual gifts, we learn what God wants us to do in and through His church. God may give you the gift of teaching. Knowing you have a gift is a wonderful revelation. However, there are many possibilities for using a gift such as teaching. Children, students, men, women and people with special needs have a desire and need to be taught. Knowing what to do is one-third of the puzzle. Knowing where to serve is based on experience.

Your life has been filled with experiences that carry over into your spiritual life. Sam loves children. His vocation is building playground equipment. Sam became a Christian and discovered that he has the gift of teaching. He is helping to teach children on the playground he built for the church. He built the playground using his gift of craftsmanship.

It would have been foolish to tell Sam to ignore his experience and teach students or adults. It would have been a mistake to ask him to ignore a vocation he loves and leave the children with the old makeshift playground.

One caution: Do not attempt to translate experiences that you do not like into the church. I once asked a painter to organize a job that needed to be done. Fortunately he was honest and told me that he did not like painting. He said that painting pays for his hobby, that was furniture building. Not long after that he constructed a series of shelves for the church.

I like the teaching of Bruce Bugbee in *Network*. Your experience (he calls it passion) is often that which could keep you awake past midnight talking about it. My defined experience is "Revising the Church." God gave me the experience as a pastor to help churches prepare for life in the twenty-first century. Prior to becoming a pastor, I reorganized two other businesses. The experience of restructuring the customer service department of a newspaper and turning a grocery store into the top in its chain has been translated into the church. God has blessed me to help organize churches by using the gifts of preaching, administration, evangelism, giving and the experience of designing churches for the future.

What experiences do you bring into the church? Look at this gift list:

Administration	Evangelism	Intercession	Prophecy
Apostleship	Faith	Interpretation	Shepherding
Craftsmanship	Giving	Knowledge	Teaching
Creative Communication	Healing	Leadership	Tongues
Discernment	Helps	Mercy	Wisdom
Encouragement	Hospitality	Miracles	

List an area or areas from your past that could impact your work within the church. 1. _____, 2. _____,

195

and 3. _____.

What leader in your church could help you to discover your spiritual gifts? _____. What leader could help you begin serving in an area you have identified? _____.
Remember to use both your experience and your gifts to find a place to serve.

The opening verse for today's study says *"Delight yourself in the LORD and he will give you the desires of your heart"* (Psalm 37:4, NIV). Most people read this and believe that it says that when we delight in God, He will give us whatever we want. It does not say that He will give us what we want, it is saying that He will place within our hearts what we should want. Delight yourself in Him, and He will place within your hearts the desire to serve according to spiritual gifts and past experiences.

Your Daily Walk

Scripture:
   Psalm 37:4

Memory verse: Remove the card that says "Psalm 37:4" from your "To Learn" group and move it to your "Working to Memorize" group. Review all your verses. See how many you know from memory.

Application:
   Talk to some leader in the church this week about how you can serve God.

Journal: _____

_____
_____
_____
_____
_____
_____
_____
_____
_____
_____
_____
_____
_____
_____
_____
_____

Prayer: _____
_____
_____
_____
_____
_____
_____

SERVE

Role - The third step to SERVE
Week 14, Day 4 - Wednesday - Date: ____/____/_____

"For you created my inmost being; you knit me together in my mother's womb. I praise you because I am fearfully and wonderfully made" (Psalm 139:13-14a, NIV).

There is a part of our lives that God knits together that defines who we are. The role you will fulfill as you serve depends on this ordained part of you. There are four possible ways you may serve. 1. You may like tasks and are structured in how you fulfill these tasks. 2. You may like tasks but want to accomplish them in an unstructured way. 3. You may like people better than tasks and like to work with people in a structured environment. 4. You may like people better than tasks and want to work with them in a free, unstructured way. You should be able to fit yourself in one of the following four quadrants.

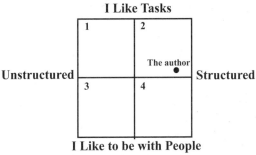

Notice where I am. I am almost off the chart toward structured. I love tasks, but I lean toward people. Through the years I have learned not to always be structured and to spend more and more time loving and encouraging people. The dot represents who I am, but learned skills allow me to venture into other areas so I can appreciate who you are.

Spiritual gifts help us know what to do. Your experience will guide you where to serve. Your role will assist you in knowing how to serve when you get where you need to be. Look at the following examples that should help you think about your role in serving within the church.

Suppose the church is organizing a women's Bible study group. The gifts of teaching, hospitality, administration, helps, creative communication, intercession and leadership would be useful. Those who have or want to have an experience with women's ministries and who have the above gifts will be helpful leaders. When the group members gather to organize a meeting, some will need to accomplish the task, while others will feel compelled to pay attention to people. There are those who will be structured and those who will serve through unstructured means.

Sarah, an unstructured hospitality leader will stand at the door and greet the women as they arrive. Jana, a structured hospitality person is making sure they get to the coffee, doughnuts and their seat. Marsha, the unstructured teacher, beautifully provides a story for the group, while Tara, the structured teacher, gives five points of application from Marsha's story.

Do you get the picture? Your life is in one of four boxes. There is no right or wrong role for you. Your role is connected to the way God beautifully made you. Where do you think you are?

Seek to serve within your role and remember to develop skills in areas where you are not particularly strong. Husbands and wives can also learn from this. Too often spouses excuse their behavior by simply saying: "That's just the way I am." When we make no attempt to develop skills in areas where we have little or no supernatural ability, we run the risk of losing our job, ministry position or even family. Your spiritual gifts and role are what you do best, but do not describe all you need to do.

Your Daily Walk

Scripture:
  Psalm 139:13-14

Application:
  What is your role?
  1. _____ Task / unstructured
  2. _____ Task / structured
  3. _____ People / unstructured
  4. _____ People / structured

Journal: _____

_____
_____
_____
_____
_____
_____
_____
_____
_____
_____
_____

Prayer: _____

_____
_____
_____
_____
_____

SERVE

*V*ision - *The fourth step to SERVE*
Week 14, Day 5 - Thursday - Date: ____/____/_____

"Where there is no vision, people perish" (Proverbs 29:18, LPP). The fourth step to serving is to get a vision from God for what He wants you to do. A vision provides focus and direction. Vision is like the banks of a river. The banks provide direction. Without the banks the mighty river turns into a miry swamp. Your vision becomes the banks of your life. Your vision provides the focus and direction of your Christian walk. It will put into motion the spiritual gifts that God has placed in you, the experience that you have gained and the personal style that defines your role. Without a vision, your service will be anemic at best and nonexistent at worst.

How do you get a vision for what God wants to do with your life? It may be helpful at this point to meet with your pastor, another minister or a church leader to discuss what you can do in the body of Christ. Explain as much as you can about your spiritual gifts, your experience and the role you might fit into. The one with whom you meet may need to read days two through four of this week to know what you have been studying and better understand how to direct you.

One of my gifts is evangelism (witnessing). In 1989 I attended an *Evangelism Explosion* Clinic at Briarwood Presbyterian Church in Birmingham, Alabama. It was one of the greatest five days of my life. I learned a gospel presentation and I learned how to organize and launch *Evangelism Explosion* in the church at which I was serving. However, the most exciting part of those six days was that I saw what Briarwood was doing and got a vision.

I got a vision for seeing hundreds saved. I got a vision for what can happen when a church walks by faith and a pastor spends an enormous amount of time in prayer. I got a vision for growing an evangelism ministry that could one day host *Evangelism Explosion* clinics. I got a vision for becoming a teacher.

I have seen hundreds saved through one church in a single year. I have experienced being the pastor of a church that walked by faith and lived by prayer. Churches I have pastored have hosted nine evangelism clinics since 1992. I became a Senior Clinic teacher for E.E. and in 1996 returned to teach the clinic at Briarwood. In 2003 God led me to write my own evangelism ministry called "*It's* LIFE." The *LIFE process* combines evangelism with the Sunday School, prayer and discipleship ministries of the church. To date, the *LIFE process* has led churches to become leaders in evangelism outreach, has helped equip other churches and has been translated into three other languages and used in three other countries. This all began with a vision.

Sometimes we learn what to do, but neglect to get a vision for doing what we learn. There are times when Christians learn what to do and get a vision, but someone in the church keeps us from accomplishing our vision. When that happens, do not give up. Go to the one who is standing in the way of what God is leading you to do. Share your concerns (in love) and pray with the person. Through prayer, God will help you to do what He called you to do.

Christians give up too easily on their vision. When we pray and persevere, we will succeed. Your vision is the channel in which your Christian life will flow. Without it you will become like a river without banks (a swamp). You will be like unwrapped dynamite powder (a big fizz). Power to serve comes from focus. It comes from your vision.

You need to find the vision that God has for you. Do not sit around and try to manufacture a vision. Your vision will be tied to your passion. On Tuesday of this week, I told you that my passion is revising the church. The vision that God gave me while at Briarwood Presbyterian Church and the subsequent work that God has done in my ministry has revised the work of the church. The book you are reading is a part of revising the church of the Lord, Jesus Christ. The evangelical church has been quick to make decisions but not disciples. The non-evangelical church has been seeking to disciple people but is hardly reaching the lost. The revised church gets a vision for reaching, baptizing, teaching, discipling and energizing. Get God's vision for your life and be an active part of revising your church.

Your Daily Walk

Scripture:
> Proverbs 29:18

Memory verse: Remove the card that says "Proverbs 29:18" from your "To Learn" group and move it to your "Working to Memorize" group. Proverbs 29:18 is your final memory verse for *More Abundant LIFE*. Keep all these cards close so that you can review and remember God's promises and instructions.

Application:
> What is your vision for serving? _____

Journal: _____

_____
_____
_____
_____
_____
_____
_____
_____
_____
_____

Prayer: _____

_____
_____
_____
_____

SERVE

Edification - The fifth step to SERVE

Week 14, Day 6 - Friday - Date: _____ / _____ / _____

"Even so you, since you are zealous for spiritual gifts, let it be for the edification of the church that you seek to excel" (1 Corinthians 14:12, NKJ).
    Edify is a biblical term that means to "build up." Christian service is designed to build up the body of Christ. Christian servants will seek to edify. There are five simple steps that you can follow that will help you to truly edify the church. Each of these steps is connected to an easy to learn and recall acrostic.

    1.   **E**ncourage people both in and outside the church as you serve. I hardly see the volunteers who manicure the forty-three acres where our church building is located. Yet every week their work encourages me and all those who both attend and drive by our physical location. We often think of encouraging people by teaching or ministering; however, true service will encourage the body of Christ no matter what we are doing.

    2.   **D**eny your pride. God gives gifts for the good of the church and reaching the world, not for self-adulation. You may become one of the best in your area of service. If you reach that pinnacle, then stand there humbly, you will stay there. Or you can leave the high ground of humility and plummet to the depths of pride. When you become boastful about who you are and receive the glory for your actions, then you are taking credit that belongs to God. The Bible says, *"Pride goes before destruction, a haughty spirit before a fall"* (Proverbs 16:18, NIV). God gave you the spiritual gifts, experience, role and vision. Be sure to give Him the credit for the accomplishments of your Christian life.

    3.   **I**ntercede for those you will serve. If you are using your gifts, you are impacting people. If you are impacting people, you need to pray. Resist the temptation to skip prayer, or you will be serving in the flesh. There are some things you may be allowed to do without seeking God's help. There is much more you will do if you pray for Him to use you to bless and bring others to Him.

    4.   **F**ree yourself. In 2 Corinthians 3:17, Paul apparently says *"Where the Spirit of the Lord is, there is liberty"* (NKJ). It was Nick "the Greek" Piravolos, author of *Too Mean to Die* who sat in my home in the 1980's, opened my Greek New Testament and said, "Lawrence, when a Greek reads this verse, the word and sentence structure translates it *"Where the Spirit of the Lord is Lord, there is liberty"* (NPP). The Spirit of the Lord is everywhere, but in those places where the Spirit of the Lord is Lord, there is freedom. The Apostle Paul was in prison, but the Spirit of the Lord was Lord over his life. In prison he was a free man. Let the Spirit of the Lord guide all you do to build up the body.

    5.   **Y**ou must **Y**ield! It is not about you, but it involves you. You must be yielded to God. Allow Him to place you where He wants you to be and move you when He wants you to move. Do something! Do not stand still. Remember you

cannot change direction with a parked car.

Christians have the powerful responsibility and privilege of serving the Creator of this universe. We are commanded to join Him in His work. Our lives begin to make an eternal impact when we see the gifts that are within us, search for the experiences of our lives that God wants to use in the future, seek to define our role in doing His work, sense His vision for our lives and edify others as we serve the body of Christ.

Relatively new Christians are often shy about seeking ways to serve within the church. Stay out of the trap of believing that you cannot serve until you are much older in Christ. You can serve now. Your service may change in the future, but, to paraphrase what Paul said to young Timothy, "Do not let anyone look down on you just because you are a young Christian, but in speech, conduct, love, faith and purity be an example to other believers" (1 Timothy 4:12, LPP). You may be a young Christian, but there are many older believers who need to see your example.

Your Daily Walk

Scripture:

2 Corinthians 3:17

Application:

Write "Lord" after the word "is" in 2 Corinthians 3:17.

Journal: _____

_____
_____
_____
_____
_____
_____
_____
_____
_____
_____
_____
_____
_____
_____
_____
_____

Prayer: _____

_____
_____
_____
_____
_____
_____

A Time to Reflect, Recover and Review
Week 14, Day 7 - Saturday - Date: _____/_____/_____

As you reflect on this week find ways to apply what God is teaching you. Review the week. Reflect on new material you have learned and insights you have gained. Return and read any material that you may have neglected to read and make journal entries on the days where you did not complete the assignments.

Be certain to make *More Abundant LIFE* your first step not your final step in your spiritual growth. My prayer for you is that one day you will come back to this book and realize the magnificent work that Christ has made in your life as you have both learned His word and put into practice what you have learned. Remember, the foundation is Jesus and the pillars of a Christian's faith that you will be building are **Prayer, Worship, Witness, Bible Study, Discipleship, Fellowship** and **Service**.

Take time to be certain you have learned the two memory verses for this week and review the memory verses from the previous weeks.

Highlights from Week 14:

Read through each day of Week 14 and record a teaching from each day:
- Monday   - _____
_____
- Tuesday   - _____
_____
- Wednesday- _____
_____
- Thursday - _____
_____
- Friday   - _____
_____

Journal:

Take time to write in your journal. Write down ideas and record events that are impacting your life in Christ. Record the victories and the struggles, the concepts you are learning and those you still do not understand.

_____
_____
_____
_____
_____

Prayer: Talk to God today. Listen to what He is saying to you.

Remember: Tomorrow is the traditional day to worship God. Whether your worship time is Friday night, Saturday or Sunday, ask God to help you to prepare before worship. Do not wait until your day of worship to rest and get ready. Prepare in advance so that you will get the most from worship.

DAY 99

As you prepare for your next study and next step of spiritual growth, allow the following testimonies to encourage you today. I pray that something similar has happened in your life.

Dear Lawrence,

At our church's new member class, I was given your book, *More Abundant Life*. I fall into the third category of readers for whom the book is written - a long-time Christian with a weak foundation. As I have sought to strengthen the seven spiritual pillars, I have been most profoundly affected by my prayer life and Bible study as a result of this reading. The very clear, methodical, thought-provoking Bible study presented in the book has led to my spending a great deal of much needed time in prayer - but specific prayer - and I have definitely felt the presence of the Holy Spirit working in my life and answering my prayers. I look forward to everything that God has planned for my life.

-Diane

Bro. Lawrence,

I want to share with you what God told me today. Today in the morning I had wonderful time with "Jo." God continues blessing Jo through the book *More Abundant Life*. We are studying this book and we will spend much more then 100 days, but The Holy Spirit is talking. Look what "Jo" said today after we studied 2 Thessalonians 3:3: "This book is a helping hand to me because in this book I learned God's words and these words make me strong to be a winner in difficult times in my life. This week is a so difficult time in my life."

-Love in Christ, *Marta* (Brazil)
(Marta's husband translated MAL
into Portuguese)

Dear Bro. Phipps,

I am writing to express my heart-felt appreciation for your book, *More Abundant Life*. I have recently finished reading it through the first 100 days. It was a kind and gracious gift from a team of three people who visited at my home. Thanks again for your ministry.

-Charles

Has God done a special work in your life during these 99 days? Write about it here: _____

_____

_____

_____

_____

If you would like to share your experience with us, then send your comments by e-mail to **lawrence.phipps@itslifeministry.com**. We will only share these in a future edition of MAL if you give us permission.

DAY 100

Monday - Date: _____/_____/_____

For ninety-nine days you have been focusing on reading what God has written and what I have written about the seven pillars of a Christian's faith. Today launches a part of your Christian walk that may not be as neatly packaged as this study was. My prayer is that you can go from the milk (what others feed you) to the meat (the ability to eat -read and study the Bible- on your own).

Today I want you to take time and try to recall and to record the greatest insights that you have gained and some of the best applications you are making to insure that each of these pillars is becoming stronger.

1. **Prayer**
   Insights: _____
   _____
   Application: _____
   _____

2. **Worship**
   Insights: _____
   _____
   Application: _____
   _____

3. **Witness**
   Insights: _____
   _____
   Application: _____
   _____

4. **Bible Study**
   Insights: _____
   _____
   Application: _____
   _____

5. **Discipleship**
   Insights: _____
   _____
   Application: _____
   _____

6. **Fellowship**
   Insights: _____

   Application: _____

7. **Service**
   Insights: _____

   Application: _____

Final thoughts:

More Abundant LIFE is not an exhaustive work of all you need to know to grow as a Christian. This book has provided some insights that will help you to begin your Christian walk. I hope that you have received enough insight to help you to have a working knowledge of the Christian faith and the Bible.

The first week I explained that Jesus is the foundation. He still is. He is deep enough, wide enough and strong enough for anything you will ever build upon Him. Now you have the seven pillars. The stronger you become in these seven areas, the larger your witness will be and the greater the contribution you will make to the Kingdom of God.

Let me leave you with my favorite verse and the first verse that you were to memorize in this study. Carry it in your heart wherever you go.

Matthew 6:33
But seek ye first the kingdom of God, and his
righteousness; and all these things shall be
added unto you. -Jesus

Endnotes

1   Lawrence H. Phipps, *Praying in FAITH*, (Copyright © 2002, LifeWay Press), p. 9.

2   Johann Tetzel, *Christendom*, (Copyright © 1964, 1966 by American Heritage Publishing Co. Inc.), p. 14.

3   D. James Kennedy, *Evangelism Explosion*, (Copyright © 1996, Fourth Edition by D. James Kennedy, Ph.D., Tyndale House Publishers, Inc.), p. 14.

4   Lawrence H. Phipps, *It's LIFE* (Copyright © 2004, For LIFE Ministries, Montgomery, Alabama), p. 15-16.

5   Lawrence H. Phipps, *Praying in FAITH*, (Copyright © 2002, LifeWay Press), p. 19.

6   Karen Phipps, *Paraphrase*, (1975), p. 68.

7   D. James Kennedy, *Evangelism Explosion*, (Copyright © 1996, Fourth Edition by D. James Kennedy, Ph.D., Tyndale House Publishers, Inc.), p. 73.

8   Lawrence H. Phipps, *Praying in FAITH*, (Copyright © 2002, LifeWay Press), p. 73.

9   Patrick Overton, *The Leaning Tree*, (Copyright © 1975, Bethany Press), p. 75.

10 Lawrence H. Phipps, *It's LIFE*, (Copyright © 2004, For LIFE Ministries, Montgomery, Alabama), p. 103.

11 Linda Lee Johnson, Claire Cloninger, Tom Fettke, *He is Lord*, (Copyright © 1986 Word Music [a division of Word, Inc.]) p. 125.

12 Max Lucado, *In the Eye of the Storm*, (Copyright © 1991, Word, Inc., Dallas, Texas), p.163.

13 Max Lucado, *In the Eye of the Storm*, (Copyright © 1991, Word, Inc., Dallas, Texas), p.163.

7

Begins on Page #

_____ in my Bible.

1

Begins on Page #

_____ in my Bible.

8

Begins on Page #

_____ in my Bible.

2

Begins on Page #

_____ in my Bible.

9

Begins on Page #

_____ in my Bible.

3

Begins on Page #

_____ in my Bible.

10

Begins on Page #

_____ in my Bible.

4

Begins on Page #

_____ in my Bible.

11

Begins on Page #

_____ in my Bible.

5

Begins on Page #

_____ in my Bible.

12

Begins on Page #

_____ in my Bible.

6

Begins on Page #

_____ in my Bible.

GENESIS
(jen' *e* s*i*s)

JUDGES
(j*u' ges)*

EXODUS
(ek' s*o* d*u*s)

RUTH
(rūth)

LEVITICUS
(l*e* v*i*t' *i* k*u*s)

1 SAMUEL
(sam' ū *e*l)

NUMBERS
(n*u*m' b*e*rz)

2 SAMUEL
(sam' ū *e*l)

DEUTERONOMY
(dōōt *er ćn' e m*ē)

1 KINGS
(kēngz)

JOSHUA
(j*o*sh' ū w*ć)*

2 KINGS
(kēngz)

19

Begins on Page #

_____ in my Bible.

13

Begins on Page #

_____ in my Bible.

20

Begins on Page #

_____ in my Bible.

14

Begins on Page #

_____ in my Bible.

21

Begins on Page #

_____ in my Bible.

15

Begins on Page #

_____ in my Bible.

22

Begins on Page #

_____ in my Bible.

16

Begins on Page #

_____ in my Bible.

23

Begins on Page #

_____ in my Bible.

17

Begins on Page #

_____ in my Bible.

24

Begins on Page #

_____ in my Bible.

18

Begins on Page #

_____ in my Bible.

1 CHRONICLES
(kron' i kulz)

PSALMS
(sćmz)

2 CHRONICLES
(kron' i kulz)

PROVERBS
(prov' erbz)

EZRA
(ez' rć)

ECCLESIASTES
(i klē' zē ćs' tēz)

NEHEMIAH
(nē' uh mī' uh)

SONG OF SOLOMON
(song) of (sćl' e men)

ESTHER
(es' ter)

ISAIAH
(ī zā' uh)

JOB
(jōb)

JEREMIAH
(jer' uh mī' uh)

31

Begins on Page #

_____ in my Bible.

25

Begins on Page #

_____ in my Bible.

32

Begins on Page #

_____ in my Bible.

26

Begins on Page #

_____ in my Bible.

33

Begins on Page #

_____ in my Bible.

27

Begins on Page #

_____ in my Bible.

34

Begins on Page #

_____ in my Bible.

28

Begins on Page #

_____ in my Bible.

35

Begins on Page #

_____ in my Bible.

29

Begins on Page #

_____ in my Bible.

36

Begins on Page #

_____ in my Bible.

30

Begins on Page #

_____ in my Bible.

LAMENTATIONS
(lĕ′ men tā′ shuns)

OBADIAH
(ō′ bu dī′ uh)

EZEKIEL
(i zē′ kē ul)

JONAH
(jō′ neh)

DANIEL
(dĕn′ yel)

MICAH
(mī′ keh)

HOSEA
(hō zā′ uh)

NAHUM
(nā′ hūm)

JOEL
(jō′ ul)

HABAKKUK
(hub ĕk′ uk)

AMOS
(ā′ mus)

ZEPHANIAH
(zef′ u nī′ uh)

43

Begins on Page #

_____ in my Bible.

37

Begins on Page #

_____ in my Bible.

44

Begins on Page #

_____ in my Bible.

38

Begins on Page #

_____ in my Bible.

45

Begins on Page #

_____ in my Bible.

39

Begins on Page #

_____ in my Bible.

46

Begins on Page #

_____ in my Bible.

40

Begins on Page #

_____ in my Bible.

47

Begins on Page #

_____ in my Bible.

41

Begins on Page #

_____ in my Bible.

48

Begins on Page #

_____ in my Bible.

42

Begins on Page #

_____ in my Bible.

HAGGAI
(hag′ ē ī′)

JOHN
(jon)

ZECHARIAH
(zek′ u rī′ uh)

ACTS
(aktz)

MALACHI
(mal′ u kī′)

ROMANS
(rō′ menz)

MATTHEW
(math′ yōō)

1 CORINTHIANS
(ku rin thē′ unz)

MARK
(mark)

2 CORINTHIANS
(ku rin thē′ unz)

LUKE
(lōōk)

GALATIANS
(gu lā′ shunz)

55

Begins on Page #
_____ in my Bible.

49

Begins on Page #
_____ in my Bible.

56

Begins on Page #
_____ in my Bible.

50

Begins on Page #
_____ in my Bible.

57

Begins on Page #
_____ in my Bible.

51

Begins on Page #
_____ in my Bible.

58

Begins on Page #
_____ in my Bible.

52

Begins on Page #
_____ in my Bible.

59

Begins on Page #
_____ in my Bible.

53

Begins on Page #
_____ in my Bible.

60

Begins on Page #
_____ in my Bible.

54

Begins on Page #
_____ in my Bible.

EPHESIANS
(i fē′ zhunz)

2 TIMOTHY
(tim′ u thē′)

PHILIPPIANS
(fi lip′ ē′ unz)

TITUS
(tī′ tus)

COLOSSIANS
(ku losh′ unz)

PHILEMON
(fil ē′ mun)

1 THESSALONIANS
(thes u lō′ nē′ unz)

HEBREWS
(hē′ brōōz)

2 THESSALONIANS
(thes u lō′ nē′ unz)

JAMES
(jāmz)

1 TIMOTHY
(tim′ u thē′)

1 PETER
(pē′ tur)

64

Begins on Page #
_____ in my Bible.

61

Begins on Page #
_____ in my Bible.

65

Begins on Page #
_____ in my Bible.

62

Begins on Page #
_____ in my Bible.

66

Begins on Page #
_____ in my Bible.

63

Begins on Page #
_____ in my Bible.

Memory Flash Card #4

Mark 11:24 (NIV)

Memory Flash Card #1

Matthew 6:33 (NKJ)

Memory Flash Card #5

Hebrews 10:25 (NIV)

Memory Flash Card #2

John 3:16 (NIV)

Memory Flash Card #6

2 Timothy 2:15 (NIV)

Memory Flash Card #3

John 10:27 (NKJ)

2 PETER
(pē′ t*u*r)

3 JOHN
(j*o*n)

1 JOHN
(j*o*n)

JUDE
(jō̄od)

2 JOHN
(j*o*n)

REVELATION
(re′ ve *l*ā′ sh*u*n)

33 But seek first the kingdom of God and His righteousness, and all these things shall be added to you.

24 Therefore I tell you, whatever you ask for in prayer, believe that you have received it, and it will be yours.

16 For God so loved the world that he gave his one and only Son, that whoever believes in him shall not perish but have eternal life.

25 Let us not give up meeting together, as some are in the habit of doing, but let us encourage one another— and all the more as you see the Day approaching.

27 My sheep hear My voice, and I know them, and they follow Me.

15 Do your best to present yourself to God as one approved, a workman who does not need to be ashamed and who correctly handles the word of truth.

Memory Flash Card #13

Ephesians 6:13-18 (NIV)

Memory Flash Card #7

Matthew 22:37-40 (NIV)

Memory Flash Card #14

Luke 14:23 (NIV)

Memory Flash Card #8

Mark 10:45 (NIV)

Memory Flash Card #15

2 Chronicles 7:14 (NKJ)

Memory Flash Card #9

Philippians 4:6 (KPP)

Memory Flash Card #16

Matthew 18:19-20 (NIV)

Memory Flash Card #10

Proverbs 3:5-6 (NIV)

Memory Flash Card #17

Romans 12:1-2 (NKV)

Memory Flash Card #11

John 16:24 (NIV)

Memory Flash Card #18

2 Corinthians 9:6 (NIV)

Memory Flash Card #12

Luke 9:23 (NIV)

37 Jesus replied: "'Love the Lord your God with all your heart and with all your soul and with all your *might.*' 38 This is the first and greatest commandment. 39 And the second is like it: 'Love your neighbor as yourself.' 40 All the Law and the Prophets hang on these two commandments."

13 Therefore put on the full armor of God, so that when the day of evil comes, you may be able to stand your ground, and after you have done everything, to stand. 14 Stand firm then, with the belt of truth buckled around your waist, with the breastplate of righteousness in place, 15 and with your feet fitted with the readiness that comes from the gospel of peace. 16 In addition to all this, take up the shield of faith, with which you can extinguish all the flaming arrows of the evil one. 17 Take the helmet of salvation and the sword of the Spirit, which is the word of God. 18 And pray in the Spirit on all occasions with all kinds of prayers and requests. With this in mind, be alert and always keep on praying for all the saints.

45 For even the Son of Man did not come to be served, but to serve, and to give his life as a ransom for many.

23 Then the master told his servant, 'Go out to the roads and country lanes and make them come in, so that my house will be full.

6 Do not worry about anything, pray about everything and thank God in advance for His answers.

14 If My people who are called by My name will humble themselves, and pray and seek My face, and turn from their wicked ways, then I will hear from heaven, and will forgive their sin and heal their land.

5 Trust in the LORD with all your heart and lean not on your own understanding; 6 in all your ways acknowledge him, and he will make your paths straight.

19 Again, I tell you that if two of you on earth agree about anything you ask for, it will be done for you by my Father in heaven. 20 For where two or three come together in my name, there am I with them.

24 Until now you have not asked for anything in my name. Ask and you will receive, and your joy will be complete.

1 I beseech you therefore, brethren, by the mercies of God, that you present your bodies a living sacrifice, holy, acceptable to God, which is your reasonable service. 2 And do not be conformed to this world, but be transformed by the renewing of your mind, that you may prove what is that good and acceptable and perfect will of God.

23 Then he said to them all: "If anyone would come after me, he must deny himself and take up his cross daily and follow me.

6 Remember this: Whoever sows sparingly will also reap sparingly, and whoever sows generously will also reap generously.

Memory Flash Card #25

Psalm 37:4 (NIV)

Memory Flash Card #19

2 Timothy 3:16 (NIV)

Memory Flash Card #26

Proverbs 29:18 (LPP)

Memory Flash Card #20

Matthew 5:13 (NIV)

Memory Flash Card #27

Ecclesiastes 4:12 (NKJ)

Memory Flash Card #21

John 15:8 (NIV)

Memory Flash Card #28

Romans 10:9-10 (NKJ)

Memory Flash Card #22

1 Corinthians 13:13 (NIV)

To Learn

(Place this card in front of and
attach to the scripture cards
with a clip.)

Memory Flash Card #23

Deuteronomy 6:5 (NIV)

Working to Memorize

(Place this card in front of and
attach to the cards as called
for twice each week.)

Memory Flash Card #24

John 13:34-35 (NKJ)

16 All Scripture is God-breathed and is useful for teaching, rebuking, correcting and training in righteousness.

4 Delight yourself in the LORD and he will give you the desires of your heart.

13 You are the salt of the earth. But if the salt loses its saltiness, how can it be made salty again? It is no longer good for anything, except to be thrown out and trampled by men.

18 Where there is no vision, people perish.

8 This is to my Father's glory, that you bear much fruit, showing yourselves to be my disciples.

12 Though one may be overpowered by another, two can withstand him. And a threefold cord is not quickly broken.

13 And now these three remain: faith, hope and love. But the greatest of these is love.

9 That if you confess with your mouth the Lord Jesus and believe in your heart that God has raised Him from the dead, you will be saved. 10 For with the heart one believes unto righteousness, and with the mouth confession is made unto salvation.

5 Love the LORD your God with all your heart and with all your soul and with all your strength.

34 A new commandment I give to you, that you love one another; as I have loved you, that you also love one another. 35 By this all will know that you are My disciples, if you have love for one another.